What Research Says to the Middle Level Practitioner

J. Howard Johnston
Glenn C. Markle

National Middle School Association

nmsa
NATIONAL MIDDLE SCHOOL ASSOCIATION

Copyright© 1986 by the NATIONAL MIDDLE SCHOOL ASSOCIATION
4807 Evanswood Drive, Columbus, Ohio 43229
Fourth Printing January 1990

ISBN 1-56090-028-8

All rights reserved. No part of this publication may be reproduced or transmitted in any form or by any means without permission in writing from the publisher except in the case of brief quotations embodied in reviews or articles.

The materials printed herein are the expressions of the authors and do not necessarily represent the policies of the NMSA.

Printed by Baesman Printing Corporation, 2120 Hardy Parkway, Cols., OH 43223

CONTENTS

Foreword iv
Preface v
I. **Organization of the Middle School** 1
    1. Middle Grade Organization 1
    2. Effective Schools 5
    3. Effective Middle Level Principals 11
    4. Teacher Behavior 16
    5. Teacher Thinking 19
    6. Teacher Stress 25
    7. Promotion & Retention 31

II. **Teaching Middle School Students** 37
    1. Motivating Students 37
    2. Classroom Management 41
    3. Classroom Groups 46
    4. Peer Relationships in the Classroom 50
    5. Ability Grouping 56
    6. Diagnostic Prescriptive Teaching 61
    7. Classroom Time 65
    8. Developing Problem Solving Skills 68
    9. Critical Thinking 73
    10. Attitude Development 78
    11. The Teacher's Effect on Pupil Self-Concept and
        Related School Performance — Part I 82
    12. Self-Concept and School Performance — Part II ... 85
    13. Instructional Questions 89
    14. Computer-Assisted Instruction 93

III. **Needed Research** 97
    1. Priorities for Research in Middle School Education 97

Foreword

Requests for permission to reprint are an indication of the value to readers of items in the *Middle School Journal*. By this measure, the column, "What Research Says to the Practitioner," ranks at the top. Since November, 1979, almost all issues of the *Journal* have contained a column prepared by Drs. J. Howard Johnston and Glenn C. Markle of the University of Cincinnati. This monograph brings these valuable columns together in a convenient and useable form.

Each column represents many hours of searching, reading, and summarizing. Not just personal opinions or the recitation of one's experiences, the articles synthesize research studies done by others. To prepare each one involved a comprehensive search of the literature, the critical reading of selected studies, distilling the findings, and the presentation of major results in a readable style. All of these tasks call for special expertise. Fortunately, both Johnston & Markle are researchers who have all of the needed specializations and competencies. Their contribution to the middle school movement through the columns and other professional activities has already been substantial. By making these rich resources readily available to the profession and the public at large through this monograph their influence will be extended still further.

As the middle school continues toward full implementation and the cry for school effectiveness is met, the light of research is needed. This monograph will provide such light and help to insure that decisions made are not just based on a personal preference or administrative convenience.

The Publications Committee is pleased to present this publication and is most grateful to the authors for sharing their considerable scholarship with us all.

John H. Lounsbury
Editor, NMSA Publications

To our children...
Kelly
Kristin
Anne
Jonas
Alex

Preface

Research is the soul of any profession. It is the accumulated scholarship of any field that records its knowledge, gives credibility to its practices, and makes public the principles and wisdom which guide professional behavior and shape professional standards. In short, research gives professionals guidance in the practice of their profession. But just as important, it gives lay people the standards by which to judge the reasonableness of a professional's actions.

In education, our practices are often squarely at odds with what our research tells us we should do. This occurs because no systematic mechanism exists for putting research findings, which come largely from university professionals, into the hands of school professionals. Even worse, research findings are seldom in a form that can be readily used by school personnel. And when research findings are presented, they are given as specific prescriptions for professional behavior, not as information that helps school professionals make sound decisions and exercise good professional judgment.

The column, "What Research Says To The Practitioner," first appeared in the *Middle School Journal* in 1979. Its purpose was to provide practicing teachers and administrators with a synthesis of the research that spoke to middle level concerns. It was not meant to be a comprehensive or exhaustive survey of the literature on each subject, nor was it designed to give *specific* rules for what school people should or should not do. Instead, we sought to present, in a non-technical and straightforward form, a discussion of research and scholarship that can be used to help school professionals arrive at good decisions about how to provide the most effective education for middle level youngsters.

Some of the topics are controversial, such as the article on ability grouping or the one on promotion and retention. Others, we are told, often produce nods of agreement as they are read by school people. All attempt to present a balanced perspective on the topic under study. Absolutely definite conclusions are few indeed. That is not so much a flaw in the research as it is a reflection of the enormous complexity of middle level education. Good research should reflect the context in which it is conducted, and because schooling goes on in many varied contexts, it is no surprise that research findings rarely present a completely unified view on a given issue. So it is the practitioner who must decide, ultimately, what is to be done on a daily basis, and those decisions are best made with attention to what we know as a profession, even if what we know isn't absolutely consistent.

Research is cumulative. No survey of research can provide a final, authoritative word on any topic. Inquiry is never closed on any issue. The reports in this book, then, are snapshots of a sort. They tell us what was known, believed and concluded at the time of their publication. Most of the findings are still reasonable and have been enhanced by more recent research.

Significant works completed since the publication of most of these columns are, of course, not included, but are recommended to the readers of this book as major contributions to the literature on middle level education. These include recent research on school effectiveness by Joan Lipsitz (*Successful Schools for Young Adolescents,* New Brunswick, N.J.: Transaction Books, 1984); James Beane and Richard Lipka's *Self-Concept, Self-Esteem, and the Curriculum* (Boston: Allyn & Bacon, 1984); the debate on brain-growth phenomena reported in the *Middle School Journal* (November, 1983; February, 1984; February, 1985, and August, 1985); David Strahan's research on adolescent thinking (*Schools in the Middle,* February, 1983; Reston; VA: NASSP); and Paul George's instructive studies of school organization and management (*The Theory Z School: Beyond Effectiveness* and *Evidence for the Middle School,* Columbus, Ohio; NMSA, 1983 and 1985). One of the most important additions to the literature in recent years has been NMSA's *Perspectives: Middle School Education, 1964-1984,* a remarkable compendium of contemporary thinking on middle level education. Recent publications by the National Association of Secondary School Principals, such as Lounsbury & Johnston's *How Fares the Ninth Grade?* (1985) and Valentine, Nickerson, Clark and Keefe's study on the effective middle level principal (Vol. I, 1981 and Vol. II, 1983), also make major contributions to our knowledge of middle level issues.

Being a professional carries with it the obligation to continually think about and reflect on what the profession believes, knows and values. We hope this volume provides you, the professional middle level educator, with some intellectual food for that thoughtful reflection.

J. Howard Johnston
Glenn C. Markle

Cincinnati, Ohio
January, 1986

I
Organization of the Middle School

1. Middle Grade Organization

School organization plans emerge for a variety of reasons. School district economics may dictate certain grade arrangements, as might a desire to achieve educational equity for minority children. Philosophical positions about the nature of schooling and the children involved may also dictate a specific arrangement, and certification laws and state standards may encourage and preserve particular grade arrangements.

At the middle level, there is a wider variation in grade arrangements than at any point in the school continuum. Valentine and his colleagues (1981) identified dozens of such arrangements with the most common being 7-8-9 (42%), 7-8 (31%), 6-7-8 (15%) and 5-6-7 (4%). In other words, approximately ninety-two percent of all middle level students find themselves in either a junior high school (a sequence of at least two grades, including the ninth) or a middle school (a sequence of at least two grades excluding the ninth). Obviously, these schools are defined by curricular and instructional differences as well, but these distinctions are not as clear as one might initially suspect; many junior high schools exhibit traits normally associated with middle schools and middle schools often exhibit characteristics akin to those of junior high schools.

The fact that two major grade organizations exist for this age student invites comparisons. At least two such comparisons are possible: those based on the curriculum and instruction provided in the school and those based on the outcomes produced by each school. Because this journal and others like it are already dedicated to exploring the organizational, curricular and instructional components of effective middle level schooling, this column will focus on the "outcomes" comparison. In other words, do junior highs and middle schools produce significantly different results? More specifically, does one organization tend to foster academic achievement, desirable student behavior, and a higher quality of student life more than the other?

After comparing the attitude and achievement of students in a middle school with those in a junior high and two elementary schools, Trauschke (1970) concluded that the students in the middle school had more favorable attitudes toward school, themselves, other students and teachers. Self-concepts were essentially the same in both settings. In the area of academic achievement, the results are more refined. Fifth and sixth graders in middle schools achieved as well as those in elementary schools, and seventh and eighth graders in middle schools performed as well as their junior high counterparts. After two years in the middle school, though, seventh and eighth grade achievement was higher for the middle school students than for the junior high students in the same grade.

Smith (1975) found that comparisons between two Ohio junior high schools, one of which employed "middle school concepts" (interdisciplinary team teaching, grouping of students based on needs, team planning for teachers, a thematic teaching approach, a discipline program managed at the team level, and an advisor-advisee program) yielded similar results. The students in the "middle school" building scored higher in reading and mathematics than did students in the junior high school that used a more traditional approach (departmentalization, non-thematic teaching, grouping by age and individual teacher planning only). In other academic areas, no differences were found, as was also the case in comparisons of student self-concept.

In a 1970 Florida study, however, Mooney found no differences in achievement among students in grades 5, 6, 7 and 8 which could be attributed to the organization of the school. Further, there were no differences in the achievement of ninth grade students enrolled in junior high schools and those who graduated from a middle school and were enrolled in the ninth grade of a high school. More important, though, Mooney revealed that attendance patterns "overwhelmingly" favored the middle schools and that their attendance "was significantly greater than in equated regular schools." Similar results were presented by Evans (1970) in his assessment of the Fort Worth middle schools. He found that middle school students scored higher than junior high students in reading and study skills, but lower in math. His analysis of attendance records, however, indicated that neither school organization could claim significantly better attendance than the other.

Sardone's 1976 study of New Jersey middle and junior high schools compared the achievement scores of 190 junior high eighth graders with those of 215 eighth graders in middle school. He concluded that the middle school youngsters outscored the junior high students on "basic skills, verbal creativity and figurative creativity." No other differences were apparent.

Not all of the research suggests even a slight edge for middle schools in academic achievement, though. Gaskill (1971) compared the achievement and attitude scores of 846 students enrolled in four middle schools with those of 381 students enrolled in two junior highs. He found that junior high students outscored middle school students (despite the unbalanced sample sizes) on total language skills, total arithmetic skills, and knowledge and use of reference materials. None of the comparisons favored the middle school, and no differences were apparent on any attitude scales or school adjustment measures.

On other measures of outcome, the results remain mixed as well. Elie (1970) compared junior high and middle school seventh and eighth graders on measures of "socio-emotional problems, self-concept and ability to learn, creative thinking ability, and physical fitness and health." She found that there were no differences between the schools except on creative thinking, where the scores favored the middle school.

Schoo (1970) compared students in 6-7-8 schools with those in 7-8-9 schools on attitude toward school, self-concept and social behavior. He found that middle school students had more positive attitudes toward school than did junior high students and that 5-6-7-8 schools seemed to provide an easier transition between elementary and middle grades than did either 6-7-8 or 7-8-9 schools.

On the other hand, Nash (1973) found that junior high males had somewhat better attitudes toward school than did middle school males, and that no other significant attitudinal differences existed. Wood (1974) found that junior high students had more positive attitudes toward schools, peers, teaching staff and instruction that did middle school students, although these conclusions were based on an imbalanced sample size which could have favored the junior high group. Fallon (1969) found no differences between junior highs and middle schools in enhancing the self-concepts of sixth and seventh grade boys, and Tobin (1969) reported no difference between junior high and middle school students in the number of problems they perceived themselves to have. Soares (1973) found that middle school students reported lower self-perceptions and had less confidence in "facing and mastering the environment."

When schools are converted from junior highs to middle schools, there are often noticeable effects. In tracing the changes that occurred during the conversion of a Tennessee school, McGee and Krajewski (1979) found that discipline referrals were cut in half, and attendance and achievement improved slightly, although the small sample size renders the finding inconclusive. Baker and Beauchamp (1975) found that, following conversion, student achievement was better for seventh and eighth graders and attitude toward school was better for all the grades of the middle school. Brantley (1982) compared student achievement scores for the period 1973-1975 when a school was a junior high to those from 1976-1981 when it operated as a middle school. He, too, found that reading and math achievement was higher under the middle school arrangement.

According to Flynn and Stone (1975), adjustment to the middle school was accomplished more quickly than adjustment to the junior high, as demonstrated by the self-concept of suburban Pennsylvania students. However, Austin (1967) found that the high school careers of middle and junior high graduates were indistinguishable from one another.

In the most exhaustive literature review yet conducted on the subject, Educational Research Service (Calhoun, 1983) concluded the following:

- There is little difference in academic achievement between middle and junior high school pupils, but neither did grade organization have any detrimental effect on the achievement of middle grade students.
- Grade organization has no apparent effect on the organizational climate of the schools.
- Studies of maturity suggest that Grade 9 students are more like tenth graders than like eighth graders. Eighth graders were, maturationally, closest to seventh graders. Neither the academic achievement nor the social development of any grade level (6, 7 or 8) appears to be affected by the arrangement in which it is housed.
- Researchers agree that the quality of the program is more important than its grade organization.
- Most research comparing junior highs and middle schools has found them more alike than different. Some researchers have concluded that, from an empirical perspective, they differ in name only.

What are we, as practitioners, to conclude from all of this? The most sensible conclusion is that we cannot expect the literature of our field to always provide definitive answers for the complex problems that educators must resolve. Rather than distaining the research for failing to give us a clear answer regarding which organizational plan is better, though, it is wiser to think of the research contribution as opening up at least two options. There is no clear evidence that one plan is better than the other; thus, either plan can be chosen with confidence. This means, of course, that school organization decisions will continue to be made on the basis of philosophical positions, economic conditions, demographics, and local preference. Research has spoken its piece and, all other things being equal (which, of course, they never are), it has told us that whether we organize our middle grades as a junior high or a middle school makes little difference. What is important is a recognition of the uniqueness of the middle level youngster and the provision of a *quality* educational program for those special boys and girls.

REFERENCES

Austin, John C. A comparative study of two forms of school organization for the early adolescent... Unpublished Ed. D. Dissertation, University of Houston, 1967.

Baker, L.G. and M.Z. Beauchamp. A study of selected variables in a change from a junior high school to a middle school, Unpublished Ed. D. Dissertation, Syracuse University, 1972.

Brantley, William E. West chester area school district middle school survey, Unpublished Report, May 1982.

Calhoun, F.D. (preparer) *Organization of the Middle Grades: A Summary of Research,* Arlington, Virginia: Educational Research Services, Inc., 1983.

Elie, Marie-Therese, A comparative study of middle school and junior high school students in terms of socio-emotional problems, self concept of ability to learn, creative thinking ability, and physical fitness and health, Unpublished Ed. D. Dissertation, Michigan State University, 1970.

Evans, Charles L. Short term assessment of the middle school plan, Fort Worth: Forth Worth Independent School District, 1970. (ED 057 091)

Fallon, J.P. A comparison of transescent male development in two organizational patterns centering on middle grade organization, Unpublished Ed. D. Dissertation, Michigan State University, 1969.

Flynn, R.V. and R.W. Stone A comparison of students' self concepts and teachers' perceptions of the individuals' self concept with rate of adjustment in a changing learning environment, *Middle School Journal,* V:1, Spring, 1975.

Gaskill, L.D. An investigation of the effects of four middle school programs upon the academic achievement and personal adjustment of eighth grade students, Unpublished Ed. D. Dissertation, North Texas State University, 1971.

Gatewood, T.E. What research says about the junior high versus the middle school, *North Central Association Quarterly,* 46:2, Fall 1971.

McGee, Jerry C. and R. Krajewski. Middle school effectiveness: a three year study, *Middle School Journal,* X:4, November 1979.

Mooney, P.F. A comparative study of achievement and attendance of 10 to 14 year olds in a middle school and in other school organizations, Unpublished Ed. D. Dissertation. University of Florida, 1970.

Nash, C.R. A comparison of student attitudes toward self, peers, teachers, principals and school environment in selected middle schools and junior high schools in mississippi, Unpublished Ed. D. Dissertation, Mississippi State University, 1974.

Sardone, N. Comparative analysis of basic skills and creativity of eighth grade students in selected junior high schools and middle schools in the state of new jersey, Unpublished Ed. D. Dissertation, Fordham University, 1976.

Schoo, P.H. Students' self-concept, social behavior and attitudes toward school in middle and junior high schools, Unpublished Ph.D. Dissertation, University of Michigan, 1970.

Smith, J. A comparison of middle school instruction and conventional instruction with respect to the academic achievement and self concept in pre and early adolescents, Unpublished Ed. D. Dissertation, University of Akron, 1975.

Soares, L.M. and others, Self perceptions of middle school pupils, *Elementary School Journal,* 73:7, April, 1973.

Tobin, W.E. Seventh grade students in two pennsylvania administrative organizations... Unpublished Ed. D. Dissertation, Pennsylvania State University, 1969.

Trauschke, Edward M. An evaluation of a middle school by a comparison of the achievement, attitudes and self concept of students in a middle school with students in other school organizations, Unpublished Ed. D. Dissertation, University of Florida, 1970.

Valentine, Jerry and others. *The Middle Level Principalship, Volume I: A Survey of Middle Level Principals and Programs,* Reston, Virginia: N.A.S.S.P., 1981.

Wood, F.H. Comparison of student attitudes in junior high and middle schools, *High School Journal,* 56:8, May, 1973.

November, 1983

2. Effective Schools*

The research on effective schools appears to comprise a formidable host. Among the most important works are those of Brookover, et al., (1979, 1983), Denham and Lieberman (1980), Edmonds (1979a, 1979b, 1981, 1978), Purkey and Smith (1982), Rutter, et al. (1979), and Vanezky (1979). These studies, however, have problems which reduce the ability to generalize on their findings, and suggest that the yield of school effectiveness research may not be as conclusive as it was thought to have been.

Purkey and Smith (1982) reported that many of the studies used different designs, methods, and measures of effectiveness which reduces the opportunity to compare findings. Comparisons would be of great value because of the limited number of schools included in the research studies undertaken. Furthermore, most of the studies relied on a "highly circumscribed, quantitative measures of school improvement based on basic skills acquisition" measured by "recording annual increases in proportionate mastery in the lowest social class." (Edmonds, 1982). Gertsten (et al., 1982) and Neufeld (1983) add that the amount of redesign effort that effective schools research has spawned well exceeds the dimensions of the original research, most of which focussed on reading and mathematics achievement exclusively.

Despite these difficulties, it would be foolish to ignore the large body of conclusions that stem from effectiveness studies. However, even these are not clearcut and mutually exclusive. As Donald Mackenzie (1983: 7-8) puts it, "There is broad agreement on the fundamental elements of effective schooling. Major constructs derive support from a variety of sources, such that the validity of many conclusions is stronger than would be warranted by the internal or external controls of any single study. At the same time, there is seldom clear agreement on the precise definition of constructs and variables in school effectiveness. The bright light of consensus around the central elements of a construct fades little by little into gray mists of uncertainty and unanswered questions at the edge. This is exactly the sort of picture one might expect, but it is also a picture that frustrates definitive summation, and resists being turned into specific recipes for school improvement."

So the problem is twofold: not only does the research yield information that may not be conclusive, but the research reviews draw conclusions from a body of evidence that "frustrates summation." Before continuing with a report of two of these summations, then, we offer the following caveat from Millikan's (1982) list of characteristics.

> THE READER SHOULD NOTE THAT SOME OF THE FINDINGS CONFLICT. THIS ONLY ENHANCES THE FACT THAT ALL THESE FINDINGS MUST BE VIEWED AS A WHOLE, AND DECISIONS MUST BE MADE ABOUT THE KINDS OF THINGS THAT ARE MOST LIKELY TO IMPACT LOCALLY. (page 2. Capitals in original.)

With that caution, one of the most comprehensive listings of effectiveness attributes is presented by Mackenzie (1983). The findings are presented on three

J.M. Ramos de Perez assisted in the preparation of this column.

dimensions: Leadership, Efficacy, and Efficiency, each with two subcategories — "core elements" and "facilitating elements." Core elements are mentioned frequently in the literature; facilitating elements may be read as specific conditions that make it easier to implement the core conditions of effective schooling. What is important about this listing is that Mackenzie suggests that there are fundamental and peripheral aspects of school effectiveness. "Installing" only the peripheral aspects is not likely to increase effectiveness.

I. Leadership dimensions
   A. Core Elements
      1. Positive climate and overall atmosphere.
      2. Goal-focussed activities toward clear, attainable and relevant objectives.
      3. Teacher directed classroom management and decision-making.
      4. Inservice staff training for effective teaching.
   B. Facilitating Elements
      1. Shared consensus on values and goals.
      2. Long-range planning and coordination.
      3. Stability and continuity of key staff.
      4. District-level support for school improvement.

II. Efficacy Dimensions
   A. Core Elements
      1. High and positive achievement expectations with a constant press for excellence.
      2. Visible rewards for academic excellence and growth.
      3. Cooperative activity and group interaction in the classroom.
      4. Total staff involvement with school improvement.
      5. Autonomy and flexibility to implement adaptive processes.
      6. Appropriate levels of difficulty for learning tasks.
      7. Teacher empathy, rapport, and personal interaction with students.
   B. Facilitating Elements.
      1. Emphasis on homework and study.
      2. Positive accountability: acceptance of responsibility for learning outcomes.
      3. Strategies to avoid nonpromotion of students.
      4. Deemphasis on strict ability grouping; interaction with more accomplished peers.

III. Efficiency Dimensions
   A. Core Elements
      1. Effective use of instructional time; amount and intensity of engagement in school learning.
      2. Orderly and disciplined school and classroom environments.
      3. Continuous diagnosis, evaluation and feedback.
      4. Well-structured classroom activities.
      5. Instruction guided by content coverage.
      6. Schoolwide emphasis on basic and higher order skills.
   B. Facilitating Elements
      1. Opportunities for individualized work.
      2. Number and variety of opportunities to learn.

By his own admission, Mackenzie's groupings may be arbitrary, but they do provide a comprehensive listing of the elements identified in the effective schools literature. A more widely distributed listing is found in Joyce, Hersh and McKibbin (1983). Their thirteen characteristics are grouped into two categories: Social Organization and Instruction and Curriculum.

The social organization category recognizes that schools are essentially social settings which are organized for a specific purpose: teaching and learning. To a large extent, the ability of the school to fulfill its function is dependent upon the quality of the social organization which prevades the building. Because the social organization of the school determines its mores, customs and "rules," effective schools have social climates which foster academic excellence. The characteristics of this kind of climate are described in the following list.

1. *Clear Academic and Social Behavior Goals.* There is a clear, schoolwide set of goals for social behavior and academic achievement. The goals are emphasized by all of the teaching staff, and there is no ambiguity about school priorities. Teachers, students, parents and administrators all share an understanding of the goals.

2. *Order and Discipline.* Teachers, students, parents and administrators agree on basic rules of conduct. At the same time, the schools are not oppressive; rules are generally positively stated, few in number and not capriciously formulated. Each rule has an obvious relationship to fostering learning.

3. *High Expectations.* Teachers and administrators hold high expectations for students. This transmits a number of messages: "we value excellence," "we think you can do it," and "you can do better than you think you can." At the same time, the expectations must be reasonable and keyed to the ability of the students.

4. *Teacher Efficacy.* Teachers believe that they can teach all of the students in their charge. Joyce says that "Efficacy is a sense of potency, and it is what provides the teacher with the psychic energy needed...to maintain a high task orientation..."

5. *Pervasive Caring.* Students know that teachers care when they express concern over incomplete assignments, when they show happiness for a job well done, and when they establish high expectations for students. One student told us that teachers care because "even when we're not around, they talk about the good things we do in their classes...they talk about us when they don't have to."

6. *Public Rewards and Incentives.* There is a system of clear, public rewards for achievement. More important, the system recognizes all forms of achievement, but focuses on academic performance.

7. *Administrative Leadership.* Principals are active in producing the conditions of effective schools. By making sure that necessary administrative tasks are carried out, the principal creates a climate wherein learning is valued, not subject to interruption and is a collective enterprise. Most important, the principal is seen as caring, supportive and trustworthy.

8. *Community Support.* Because effective schools have more contacts with parents and community members, the community tends to support school goals and believe that the school is doing a good job in achieving them. Parents and other community members are frequently involved in meaningful school activities: tutoring, fund-raising, planning, and the like.

Differences between the curriculum and instruction in effective schools and those of less effective schools are quite distinct. Among the most prominent features of the *academic* program of effective schools are the following.

1. *High Academic Learning Time.* The very best schools provide high quality academic time for a large portion of the school day. The instruction engages student attention, and functions at a level appropriate to the individual student. In the most effective schools, students enjoy a high rate of success (90 percent or better) — a product of student effort and the proper selection of learning tasks for the child.

2. *Frequent and Monitored Homework.* Out of class assignments tend to increase academic learning time, provided that it is neither trivial nor too difficult. It tells the student that learning continues outside of school, and that independent effort is required for real learning to take place. Most important, effective schools monitor homework — not just its completion, but its content and quality. Students get regular and complete feedback on their work in these schools, indicating that the work they do is important and worth the teacher's time to examine.

3. *Coherently Organized Curriculum.* Not surprisingly, effective schools have curricula that are organized around the commonly-agreed upon goals of the school. Commercially prepared materials are used, but are not in abundance — the preference seems to be for teacher made materials or teacher adaptations of commercial materials. Obviously, there is also a close match between what is taught and what is tested.

4. *Variety of Teaching Strategies.* Teachers in effective schools use a variety of teaching strategies, thereby allowing them to better accommodate individual differences. They are well-equipped to resort to another strategy when any student is not progressing as expected.

5. *Opportunities for Student Responsibility.* Students are given the opportunity to act responsibly and with good judgment. They are given criteria by which to evaluate their behavior, and are encouraged to assess their own performance.

Other investigations (Johnston and Perez, 1984; Lipsitz, 1983) undertaken using naturalistic methods to study the academic culture of effective middle level schools confirm the presence of the foregoing list of characteristics in middle level schools as well. However, additional characteristics appear to be unique to middle level schools.

Lipsitz's major conclusions are telling for their emphasis upon the quality of life in the school. She found that they were willing and able to adapt school practices to the "individual differences in intellectual, biological and social maturation of their students." Furthermore, the positive climates that permeated the schools were established for their intrinsic worth, not just as means to academic goals. Academically, the effective schools Lipsitz studied had "achieved unusual clarity about the purpose of intermediate schooling and the students they teach." The experience was not seen just as a point between the formative experiences of elementary school and the preparation for adulthood of the high school. Interestingly, though, most of the principals in Lipsitz's schools had elementary backgrounds, and most of the teachers tended to identify their schools more as elementary than secondary in nature.

In the effective schools studied by Johnston and Perez, most of Lipsitz's findings were confirmed, and additional conclusions were drawn. Academically, the climate of the school encouraged the pursuit of academic activity outside of formal class structures. Students were often engaged in conversations about academic matters, teachers and students often talked about some problem or academic question not as an instructional approach, but out of genuine curiosity, and special activities, such as rocket launchings and "Olympics of the Mind" competitions were organized to imbue the school's social life with an academic emphasis.

Students and teachers in the best schools knew how to influence school policy and believed that they could. Usually, they had the most confidence in informal influence mechanisms, and rather than going to the student council with a problem, were more likely to "talk with the principal" about any given issue.

Most important, according to Johnston and Perez, is the fact that the schools were trusting places. Students and teachers were trusted to behave in productive, civil ways, so there was no need for enormous listings of rules which dealt with every conceivable infraction. That, they concluded, only encourages legalistic thinking: "If there's no rule against it, it must be O.K."

Despite the appeal of using these lists of effectiveness attributes as prescriptions for school improvement, it is important that we recognize that *these characteristics appear in schools which are effective; they are not necessarily the elements that make the school an effective one.* The message in this conclusion is that one cannot install a school effectiveness program. Effective schools emerge from a complex set of cultural and social factors that focus attention on academic performance, support academic growth in a manner consistent with the developmental stage of the youngster, and build an intellectual community that rewards and reinforces academic pursuits in its public rituals and in its private interactions. It is the creation of this culture, not the installation of the major characteristics of effective schools, that will enhance student learning and produce long-term school improvements.

References

Beane, J. and R. Lipka. *Self concept, self esteem and the curriculum,* Boston: Allyn and Bacon, 1984.
Brookover, W., et al., *School social systems and student achievement: Schools can make a difference,* New York: Praeger, 1979.
Brookover, W., et al., *Creating effective schools,* Holmes Beach: Learning Publications, 1983.
Denham, C. and A. Lieberman, *Time to learn,* Washington: U.S. Department of Health, Education and Welfare, National Institute of Education, 1980.
Edmonds, R. A discussion of the literature and issues related to effective schooling. Cambridge: Center for Urban Studies, Harvard Graduate School of Education, 1979(a).
Edmonds, R. Effective schools for the urban poor. *Educational Leadership,* 1979(b), 37, 15-27.
Edmonds, R. Making public school effective, *Social Policy,* 1981, 12 (2), 56-60.
Edmonds, R. and J.R. Frederiksen, *Search for effective schools: the identification and analysis of city schools that are instructionally effective for poor children.* Cambridge: Center for Urban Studies, 1978,
Gersten, R., et al., The principal as instructional leader: a second look *Educational Leadership,* 1982, 40 (3), 47-50.
Johnston, J.H. and J.M. Ramos de Perez, The four climates of effective middle level schools, paper presented at the Middle School Invitational, National College of Education, Chicago, Illinois, November, 1983.
Joyce, B., R.H. Hersh, and M. McKibbin, *The structure of school improvement,* New York: Longman, 1983.
Lipsitz, J.S. *Successful schools for young adolescents,* New Brunswick: Transaction Books, 1983.
Mackenzie, D. Research for school improvement: an appraisal of some recent trends, *Educational Researcher,* 1983, 12 (4), 5-17.
Millikan, T. *Approaching the research on effective schools and effective classrooms,* Harrisburg; Pennsylvania Department of Education, May, 1982.
Neufeld, B., et al., A review of effective schools research: the message for secondary schools, Cambridge: the Huron Institute, 1983 (ERIC ED 228-241).
Purkey, W. and M. Smith, Too soon to cheer? Synthesis of research on effective schools. *Educational Leadership,* 1982, 40 (3), 64-69.

Rutter, M., et al., *Fifteen thousand hours: secondary schools and their effects on children,* Cambridge: Harvard University Press, 1979.

Vanezky, R., and L.F. Winfield. *Schools that succeed beyond expectations in teaching.* (Studies in Education Technical Report No. 1.), Newark: University of Delaware, 1979.

August, 1984

3. Effective Middle Level Principals*

Periodically, the attention of the American people is focused on educational excellence. Since quite early in its history, the middle level school has been the object of special attention, beginning with the recommendations of the Committee of Ten at the turn of the century and culminating with the extrapolation of recommendations for middle level education from *A Nation At Risk,* essentially a high school document. Such generalization of findings from one school setting to another has been a common fact of middle level education, and the recommendations of reports such as *A Nation At Risk* persist for years.

In 1918, the Bureau of Education's Commission on the Reorganization of Secondary Education produced the "Cardinal Principles of Secondary Education" which provided an expanded set of goals for secondary education that was to guide middle and secondary level policy and practice for nearly 50 years. The commission saw health, command of fundamental processes, worthy home membership, vocation, citizenship, valuable use of leisure time, and the development of ethical character as the main objectives of education.

Half a century later, the American Association of School Administrators (1966) identified similar objectives in their "Nine Imperatives for Education." These Imperatives cover three areas of development: intellectual, social and emotional. Most middle school curricula today reflect specific attention to each of these areas of human development, and recognize the especially volatile nature of our young adolescent clients. Most school leaders would argue that all three sets of objectives are of equal importance and must be given attention.

One needn't read very far in the research on effective schools, though, to see that much of the research has focused exclusively on one of these areas of endeavor: the intellectual domain. While this is obviously to the detriment of the other developmental tasks the school is held accountable for, another potentially more serious problem is evident in this research as well. Most of it is restricted to studies of students at the lower end of the socio-economic scale, and to students in need of remedial education. Ron Edmonds (1972) has written "The criticism of the education status quo that motivates school improvement efforts fixes on academic mastery among low income children. Designs for school improvement, therefore, focus on basic skill acquisition and measure gain by recording annual increases in proportionate mastery in the lowest social class. This is a highly circumscribed, quantitative measure of school improvement." And while some of these criticisms have been rectified somewhat in later research, the emphasis remains fixed, squarely, on the incremental gain in achievement test scores as a measure of school effectiveness, virtually ignoring the other responsibilities of the school.

School effectiveness is a complex question at best. The results of research are sometimes contradictory, and often dependent upon the theoretical orientation of the researchers; the criteria for selection of effective schools are often open to debate; and the manner in which data are collected and analyzed are, as in all research studies, frequently discussed at length. What is the school practitioner to make of all of this? That is the question this review of effective schools

*Denis Forrer assisted in the preparation of this column.

attempts to answer. In this column, we will examine *the role of effective leadership* on the creation and maintenance of an effective school.

Almost without exception, the major studies and reviews of school effectiveness, regardless of the operational definition of effectiveness that is employed or the theoretical orientations of the researchers, have identified the principal as a strong performer in achieving educational excellence. Taking this point of agreement as a place to begin, this column will examine different conceptions of the effective middle level leader in an effort to synthesize the findings for school practitioners.

Because leadership is regarded as one of the major determinants of the effective school, it is to be expected that there is a close correlation between the leadership behaviors regarded as necessary for effective schools and the behaviors actually demonstrated by the principal in schools that have been identified as effective. For the most part, this correlation is well founded.

Keedy and Achilles (1982) identified three distinct leadership behaviors related to norm-setting that have been linked to school effectiveness. These include setting high standards for performance of teachers, setting high expectation for students by working with teachers, and coordinating and sequencing school-wide goals and objectives. Implicit in this list, of course, is the expectation that the principal has also seen to the development of school-wide goals and objectives that enjoy widespread consensus among the professional staff and the students.

In the same study, the authors identified four ways in which principals establish norms they deem appropriate for their buildings. First, they provide appropriate resources. Expectations which have no chance of being fulfilled because resources aren't available to support their achievement are not expectations at all — they are dreams. But neither are resources always financial. Often, the resources needed are time, professional support and a warm, caring environment.

Second, norms are reinforced when relationships between the teachers and the principal and among the professional staff are such that teachers and students *want* to comply with them. In other words, norms are not enforced by some arbitrarily derived authority; they are enforced by members of the norm group because the relationships among group members are too precious to sacrifice to nonconformity.

Third, norms are reinforced when the principal uses "position power," or the preceived authority of his or her office, to support norm behavior. Most often, this is achieved by using rewards and recognition to reinforce desirable behavior. Norm-referenced behavior usually cannot be dictated, because that requires the establishment of authority that places the principal outside of the group which actually establishes and enforces norms for group behavior.

Finally, strong leaders model desirable behavior either consciously or unconsciously. The behavior of the principal (toward teachers, students, parents, etc.) sets the "norm" for the building and communicates very clearly that "this must be what's expected. After all, it's what *s/he* does."

The following characteristics of effective principals are regularly cited in the literature, albeit often with limited empirical research to support the claims. In a sense, they are the abilities required to establish the norm setting behaviors referred to by Keedy and Achilles. (Space restrictions prohibit a complete listing of the 40 articles from which this conclusion is drawn. A complete list is available from the authors.)

These abilities can be summarized quite succinctly as follows. The effective leader has the ability to
(1) develop appropriate goals,
(2) monitor and evaluate school programs in accordance with those goals,
(3) work closely with others in a consultative fashion,
(4) provide instructional support and staff support through supervision, inservice and other professional growth activities.

Perhaps most important, the effective principal is a team leader who displays high levels of interpersonal skill and is especially adept at communicating with all levels both inside and outside of the school system. The principal must be available to all parties, must involve all members of the school in the educational process, and must seek meaningful input from all members of the community served by the school.

At the risk of triteness, the image that emerges is a principal who is less the busy manager than s/he is a nurturing, consultative communicator. Authority is less important than skill at building consensus.

In the most comprehensive study of effective middle level leadership to date, the National Association of Secondary School Principals, with the support of the Geraldine R. Dodge Foundation, examined the behaviors and beliefs of fifty principals of schools selected because of their excellence by a panel of experts. The researchers, James W. Keefe, Donald C. Clark, Neal C. Nickerson, Jr. and Jerry Valentine, developed a comprehensive profile of the effective middle level principal which is presented in volume II of their study, *The Effective Middle Level Principal* (1983).

Principals were rated on five criteria:
(1) The appropriateness of the philosophy and the goals of the school and the success of the leadership in implementing them;
(2) the success of the principal in implementing individualized programs for students;
(3) leadership efforts to develop a positive school climate;
(4) the ability to anticipate problems and act to resolve them; and
(5) the level of involvement of the community in school affairs.

Data for the study were collected from questionnaires, school visits, and interviews with principals, staff, students, and parents.

The effective principals were slightly older and more experienced as principals than the national sample of principals surveyed in 1981. Their major strengths were in human relations skills, communication skills, availability, and a firm but humane control of students and schools. The effective principal values his or her work and is seen as a good problem solver by teachers and parents. In almost all cases, the principals see themselves as they are seen by the community — there is high congruence between the principal's perception of him or herself and the view of the school and community.

Effective principals are professional, democratic, and have a high degree of "people orientation," as well as a concern for task accomplishment. Therefore, it is to be expected that these principals are rated as extremely effective in staff relations. They emphasize open communication and teacher participation, and they actively involve the staff in decision making. This productive relationship extends to students, parents and other community members and groups. The principals were knowledgeable about the majority of key educational issues impinging on the schools, and they were perceived as the leading change agents in the schools. Finally, they were regarded as highly effective facilitators — helping things happen and helping others bring their ideas to fruition.

The following table shows the characteristics observed in the N.A.S.S.P.'s effective middle level principal study as they relate to characteristics of effectiveness cited in the literature.

PRINCIPAL EFFECTIVENESS AND LEADERSHIP BEHAVIOR

Effective Principals	Leadership Characteristics
High academic goals	Develops appropriate goals Monitors, evaluates program Monitors, evaluates staff Sets instructional strategies Sets high expectations
Person oriented	Interpersonal skills Available
Relates to students	Interpersonal skills
Caring	Interpersonal skills Available
Strong communicator	Works closely with others Interpersonal skills Effective communicator
Accessible	Available
Democratic leader	Uses "team" approaches Shares responsibility Shares power
High task orientation	Develops appropriate goals Monitors, evaluates program Monitors, evaluates staff Monitors use of time Sets instructional strategies Sets high expectations
Good working relationship with staff	Works closely with others Uses "team" approaches Shares responsibility Shares power Interpersonal skill Effective communicator
Administers rules fairly	Is flexible and adjustable
Regularly meets parents	Involves community Effective communicator
Has role in curriculum development	Monitors, evaluates program Provides staff support Assists in professional growth Develops appropriate goals Organizes the environment Sets instructional strategies

High rate of inservice	Monitors, evaluates staff
	Assists in professional growth
Teachers feel prepared	Monitors, evaluates staff
	Assists in professional growth

There is a strong correlation between the attributes of leadership identified in the literature and the behaviors actually exhibited by effective middle level principals. In fact, apart from per capita expenditures and pupil/teacher ratios, nearly all other requirements for school effectiveness rely to some extent on the principal.

But the effective principal is only one ingredient in the complex culture that produces an effective school. And while she or he has much to do with other elements of the effective school, it is important to study those as well. Otherwise, the success or failure of a school depends too heavily upon the professional and interpersonal competence of a single person. That, in any complex organization, is unproductive.

REFERENCES

American Association of School Administrators, Commission on Imperatives of Education, *Imperatives of Education*, Washington: AASA, 1966.

Bureau of Education Bulletin, No. 35, *Cardinal Principles of Secondary Education*, Washington: Department of the Interior, 1918.

Edmonds, Ronald R. Program of school improvement: an overview, paper prepared for the National Institute of Education, February 1982.

Keedy, John L. and Charles M. Achilles, Principal norm setting as a component of effective schools, paper presented to the Southern Regional Council on Educational Administration, Atlanta, Georgia, November 16, 1982.

Keefe, James W., Donald C. Clark, Neal C. Nickerson, Jr., and Jerry Valentine, *The Middle Level Principalship, Volume II: The Effective Principal*, Reston, Virginia: The National Association of Secondary School Principals, 1983.

May, 1984

4. Teacher Behavior

Middle school teachers are generally conscientious and desire to operate as effectively as possible in the classroom. Administrators want to hire teachers with the greatest potential for success, and colleges and universities preparing teachers want to graduate high quality candidates to fill teaching positions.

A problem facing each of these groups resides in the question, "What makes an effective middle school teacher?" While answers to this question can be, and have been, suggested by practitioners in the field (4, 16), empirical data related to this issue have also been collected and analyzed. The purpose of this report, then, is to summarize what *researchers* conclude to be the characteristics and practices of effective middle school teachers.

After reading this summary, you may want to compare your own performance to these desired, "empirically supported" teaching practices. It is hoped such self-analysis will result in improved instructional practices in middle school classrooms.

In the growing body of research on teacher effects, the most useful findings are those which address "clusters" of related teacher behaviors rather than single, isolated behaviors. In fact, the complex interactions that exist among teacher behaviors should render as suspect those reports which prescribe *specific* behaviors, practiced in isolation from other considerations. So that the reader can enjoy some confidence in the conclusions reported here, teacher behaviors have been clustered under a variety of competency headings. In each case, indicators of the competency, as derived from research, are listed.

Effective middle school teachers...

1. ...*have a positive self concept* (1, 6, 5, 17). They identify with others, feel adequate, trust themselves, and see themselves as worthy and likeable. They need not be the center of attention at all times, and are comfortable letting the classroom activities or the students themselves take precedent some of the time.
2. ...*demonstrate warmth* (7, 17). Teachers who seek contact with students, use affectionate words, smile and look pleasant are generally regarded as more effective. Teacher displays of warmth are important because teachers who like students (and show it) tend to have students who like each other.
3. ...*are optimistic* (17). More effective teachers express positive attitudes and pleasant feelings in the classroom. They are optimistic in their assessments of indivudual student capabilities and tend to be encouraging.
4. ...*are enthusiastic* (13). Effective teachers are vigorous in their presentations and involved in the activities of the class. They tend to gesture and avoid "reading" prepared lessons.
5. ...*are flexible* (17). These teachers can change the focus in the middle of a lesson if the students become bored or disinterested; they adjust easily to changes in plans, time schedules, absence or student behavior; they respond to constructive requests for changes in classroom procedure.
6. ...*are spontaneous* (17). Spontaneous teachers can capitalize on unexpected incidents that arise in class. They also tend to encourage student expression and do not avoid situations which deviate from planned activities.

7. ...*accept students* (14,17). Accepting teachers avoid criticism, not refusing to tell a student he or she is wrong, but by using sincere and frequent statements of approval. These teachers are disinclined to berate or belittle children in front of others or to display negative perceptions publicly.
8. ...*demonstrate awareness of developmental levels* (17). They assign tasks appropriate to a student's ability and adjust tasks when students become confused or uncertain. They show less tendency to push students into activities for which they are not ready, and they express less bewilderment over student inability to perform tasks.
9. ...*demonstrate knowledge of subject matter* (17). Knowledgeable teachers are able to structure lessons and alter instruction on the basis of student needs. They are able to monitor learning and engage students in instructional activities related to significant concepts.
10. ...*use a variety of instructional activities and materials* (12, 14). These teachers are able to vary instruction in accordance with individual student learning styles.
11. ...*structure instruction* (12, 17). Teachers who spend time discussing, explaining and stimulating cognitive processes in organized ways encourage greater pupil performance. They tend to review previous lessons, outlining main topics of planned lessons, signalling the beginnings and endings of lessons, underscoring important points and summarizing. These teachers are less likely to begin lessons without organizing them, change activities abruptly, or begin new topics without summarizing previous ones.
12. ...*monitor learning* (17). These teachers check test papers and student work in order to adjust instruction. They also move about the room, observing students and making suggestions. In lieu of "busy work," they used extra time for creative, social or interest-directed activities.
13. ...*use concrete materials and focused learning strategies* (11). These teachers use models, objects and visual aids to provoke imagery; attend to the manipulation of concrete images before moving to formal operations; and focus student attention on problem-solving situations.
14. ...*ask varied questions* (10, 13, 17). Using both higher order and lower order questions, in appropriate situations, produces improved student performance. Using a variety of question types for maximizing instructional effectiveness is preferable to relying on a single type of question.
15. ...*incorporate indirectness in teaching* (15, 7). Indirect teachers build on student statements, praise students, encourage student talk, and minimize criticism, lecture and confusion.
16. ...*incorporate "success-building" behavior in teaching* (18, 17). Success-oriented teachers use positive reinforcers, encouragement, and praise of student work. They are disinclined to use sarcasm, shame and harrassment.
17. ...*diagnose individual learning needs and prescribe individual instruction* (17). More effective teachers monitor the completion of tasks, perceive various learning rates and allow adequate time for completion. They design interest-based learning tasks, define expectations on an individual basis, and allow for independent and small group activities. They also demonstrate less of a tendency to teach an entire class the same lesson and to grade on a group standard.

18. ...*listen* (1, 17). Teachers who listen to students attend to and build upon student thoughts and expressions. They acknowledge student input by summarizing what was said and by avoiding the appearance of preoccupation.

The image of the competent middle school teacher that emerges from this research is thus a self-confident "personable" professional who demonstrates awareness of both student needs and varied learning strategies. While this image is not unlike that which emerges from "arm chair" listings of competencies, this image has the added validity of empirical research. Hopefully, as the research base grows more detailed, the lines of the image will grow more distinct.

REFERENCES
1. Aspy, David N. and Buhler, June H. The effect of teacher's inferred self concept upon student achievement, *The Journal of Educational Research*, Volume 86, pp. 3865-389.
2. Brophy, Jere E. Reflections on research in elementary schools, *Journal of Teacher Education*, Volume XXVII, Number 1, (Spring 1976), pp. 31-34.
3. Clarizio, Harvey F., Craig, Robert C., and Mehrens, William A. *Contemporary issues in educational psychology.* Boston: Allyn and Bacon, Inc., 1977.
4. Colorado Junior High/Middle School Executives Position Paper, Spring, 1973.
5. Combs, Arthur W., Blume, Robert A. Newman, Arthur J., and Wass, Hannelore L. *The professional education of teachers.* Boston: Allyn and Bacon, Inc., 1974.
6. Edeburn, Carl E. and Landry, Richard G. "Teacher self concept and student self concept in grades 3, 4, and 5." *The Journal of Educational Research*, Volume 69, 372-375.
7. Gage, N.L. *Teacher effectiveness and teacher education.* Palo Alto, California: Pacific Books, 1972.
8. Gage, N.. The yield of research on teaching, *Phi Delta Kappan*, Volume 60, Number 3 (November 1978), pp. 229-235.
9. Gage, N.L. and Winne, Philip H. Performance-based teacher education", in *Teacher Education*, ed. Kevin Ryan. Chicago: The University of Chicago Press, 1975.
10. Gall, Meredith D. and Joyce P. The discussion method, in *The psychology of teaching methods*, ed. N.L. Gage. Chicago: The University of Chicago Press, 1976, pp. 196-204.
11. Goode, Thomas L., Biddle, Bruce J., and Brophy, Jere E. *Teachers make a difference.* New York: Holt, Rinehart and Winston, 1975.
12. McDonald, Frederick J. Report on phase II of the beginning teacher evaluation study, *Journal of Teacher Education*, Volume XXVII: 39-42, 1976.
13. Rosenshine, Barak. Recent research on teaching behaviors and student achievement," *The Journal of Teacher Education*, Volume XXVII; 61-64, 1976.
14. Rosenshine, Barak and Furst, Norma. Research on teacher performance criteria, in *Research on Teacher Educaton*, class handout.
15. Soar, Robert. Teaching behavior related to pupil growth, *International Review of Education*, 18. 508-525.
16. Teacher Education Advisory Council, State of Florida, as published in *National Elementary Principal*, November 1971.
17. Tikunoff, William J., Berliner, David C., and Rist, Ray. *Special Study A: an ethnographic study of the forty classrooms of the beginning teacher evaluation study known sample.* San Francisco: Far West Laboratory for Education Research and Development, 1975.
18. Van Horn, Royal. Effects of the use of four types of teaching models on student self-concept of academic ability and attitude toward the teacher, *American Educational Research Journal*, Fall 1976.

May, 1979

5. Teacher Thinking*

Educational theorists, curriculum specialists, classroom management experts, textbook writers, educational researchers and school administrators share a common bond. The common bond is that there is nothing they can do to affect the classroom learning environment which is not mediated by the classroom teacher. For this reason, and others, there is a new trend in educational research, the focus of which is the study of teacher thinking.

Teacher thinking research is, in part, a reaction to the scientific study of teacher behavior. Gage (1963), in an effort to develop a paradigm for educational research, proposed the study of the relationship between teacher behavior and student achievement. This research has been referred to as teacher effectiveness research or process-product research. A major assumption of teacher effectiveness research is that teacher behavior is directly related to student achievement. The goal, therefore, of teacher effectiveness research is to identify "effective" teacher behavior and get teachers to act in "effective" ways to produce greater student achievement. The scientific study of teacher behavior has been helpful to a certain extent, especially in providing information about how to teach *low-level factual knowledge*, but researchers in the area of teacher thinking argue that teaching is much more of an art than a science.

The problem with viewing teaching as a collection of specific behaviors is the assumption that researchers will be able to identify all the effective behaviors teachers need to exhibit and that teachers will then simply learn the appropriate practices. Clark (1983) has argued that teachers are much more than mere technicians, they are more like professionals emersed in a complex learning environment, who draw on all their past experience to negotiate the maze of the classroom. Clark writes:

> Research-based knowledge, no matter what its quality or extensiveness, will never provide a complete and sufficient basis for teacher education or for the practice of teaching. Research can help us think about teaching and teacher preparation more clearly, but these professions have fundamentally practical, clinical, and artistic dimensions that exceed the scope of the social and behavorial sciences. Excellence in teaching and teacher preparation are not puzzles to be solved once and for all by a research breakthrough. Rather, they are ideals to be pursued continually by dedicated professionals who draw upon all of their knowledge, insight, imagination, and creativity to make the most of an ever-changing present (p.5).

There are other reasons for the study of teacher thinking. Elbaz (1983) suggests that teachers are generally the recipients of educational "cures" that come from researchers and administrators. Teachers tend to be resentful and argue that administrators and university personnel don't remember what it was like when they were in the classroom. "Too frequently the emphasis was on diagnosing teacher failings and on prescribing improvements" (p. 4). The teacher is seen only as "a cog in the educational machine" (p. 10). Elbaz asserts that researchers need to understand classrooms from the teacher's point of view. Only with this

---

*James A. Boland assisted in the preparation of this column.

understanding can we hope to improve the art of teaching and the education of pre-service teachers. Clark and Peterson (1984) write, "The ultimate goal of research...is to construct a portrayal of the cognitive psychology of teaching for use by educational theorists, researchers, policy makers, curriculum designers, teacher educators, school administrators, and teachers themselves" (p. 2). The purpose of this column is to review the research on teacher thinking and examine what the results say to the practitioner.

The Yield of Teacher Thinking Research

Clark (1983) reports that much of the impetus for teacher thinking research grew out of the National Conference on Studies in Teaching convened by the National Institute of Education (NIE). The report issued by Panel 6, a diverse group of experts considering the topic, "Teaching as Clinical Information Processing," provided a rationale for the study of teacher thinking. The report stated, "it will be necessary for an innovation in the context, practices, and technology of teaching to be mediated through the minds and motives of teachers."

Research in teacher thinking encompasses a number of subcategories of research. These include *teacher planning, teacher's interactive thoughts and decisions,* and *teachers' implicit theories.* The remainder of the column will focus on these three areas.

Teacher Planning

The typical model of teacher planning includes:
1. Specify objectives
2. Select learning activities
3. Organize learning activities
4. Specify evaluation procedures.

The model of planning outlined above was developed by Tyler (1950) and elaborated upon by Taba (1962) and Popham and Baker (1970). Clark and Yinger (1977) have referred to this model as the Rational Ends-Means Model. In this model, "curriculum planning is characterized as a task that required orderly and careful thinking and this model is proposed as a rational and scientific method for accomplishing this task" (p. 281). The research emphasis in this model is to develop scientific principles on which sound teaching sould be based. Newer models of planning, on the other hand, don't fit into the scientific camp.

There is a growing belief that the above model for planning and curriculum design is not an appropriate one for the classroom. Zahorik (1975), Macdonald (1965), and Macdonald, Wolfson and Zaret (1973) have proposed alternative conceptions of how teachers go about planning. One alternative model to the Rational Ends-Means Model is the Integrated Ends-Means Model proposed by Macdonald (1965) and Eisener (1967). Clark and Yinger (1977), in an early review of the research on teacher thinking, suggest that when teachers go about the business of planning, they think not of objectives but of activities. The most basic unit of planning is the activity and objectives only arise within activities, once students choose their own learning experiences and pursue their own objectives. "Thus, in this model, ends for learning became integrated with means for learning and specification of goals prior to an activity become meaningless" (p. 281). The point here is that teachers and students will always have enormous effects on the instructional process that could not have been seen beforehand. Students and teachers, drawing on their own subjective experience, will influence the learning process in such a way that instruction meets their own needs regardless of the pre-specified objectives.

Zahorik (1975) analyzed "what teachers actually do as they prepare to teach" (p. 134). The teachers were asked to list in writing the decisions they usually make before teaching. Eight categories were used to classify the decisions: objectives, content, activities, materials, diagnosis, evaluation, instruction, and organization. Zahorik reports, "that no type of decision was made by all teachers. The decision that came closest to being used by all teachers was activities. This decision was made in 81 percent of the plans" (p. 136). Zahorik does suggest, however, that teachers do not seem to be using the Integrated Ends-Means Model because they do not start the planning process by thinking of activities.

Yinger (1980), using participant observation, conducted a study of the planning of a single teacher. Yinger spent five months observing and taking notes on the planning processes of a teacher in a first-second grade "split" classroom. He found two central aspects of the teacher's planning and instruction: activities and routines. Nearly all of the interaction which took place in the course of a day occurred during planned routines. Occasionally these new activities became routinized. Based on this research, Yinger developed a new model of teacher planning.

Yinger referred to this model as the General-Process Model which was based on discovery and design rather than choice. This model of teacher planning has three stages: problem-finding; problem formulation/solution; and implementation, evaluation, and routinization. Clark and Peterson (1984) have written:

> A significant contribution of Yinger's way of conceptualizing the planning process is that he proposes a cyclical rather than a linear model. He postulates a recursive design cycle similar to the processes hypothesized to go on in the work of architects, physicians, artists, designers, and other professionals. In addition, he acknowledges that schooling is not a series of unrelated planning-teaching episodes, but that each planning event can be influenced by prior planning and teaching experiences and that, potentially, each teaching event feeds into future planning and teaching processes. He represents the cycle as a continuous, year-long process, in which the boundaries between planning, teaching, and reflection are not sharp and distinct (p. 34).

These findings correspond rather closely to work done by other researchers who have spent a long period of time with one teacher. Elbaz (1983) found that the teacher she studied, Sarah, failed to use a linear, rational model of planning. Instead, Sara chose

> among alternative materials, deciding how to adapt programs to the needs of particular classes, combining materials to make up new curriculum packages, writing units and complete programs, and putting them into use in the classroom. Materials often require further modification in the light of student response, or diverse uses to meet the needs of individual students. Sometimes carefully made plans are thrown out the window in order to respond to one of the fleeting opportunities that classroom life offers (p. 4-5).

This understanding has led other researchers to study how and when teachers make decisions which lead them away from their original plans. The research on teacher interactive decision making, is interested in learning about when teachers continue with planned activities and when they move on to take advantage of opportunities that arise in the context of teaching.

Teacher Interactive Decision Making

As one might guess, it isn't easy to measure teacher decision making, especially while they're teaching. Researchers have used a number of techniques to get at the thought processes of teachers. What these techniques generally have in common is they use some form of stimulated recall to help teachers remember what they were focusing on when they were teaching. Audiotaping or videotaping is frequently used in this research paradigm.

Peterson and Clark (1978), using videotapes of instruction as stimulated recall, reported on the interactive thought processes of teachers during teaching. Peterson and Clark had teachers view the first 2 to 3 minute segment of their teaching, the last 2 to 3 minute segment and a 2 to 3 minute segment randomly selected from the middle of the videotape. After viewing the videotape, the teachers were asked the following four questions in a structured interview:
1. What are you doing in this segment and why?
2. What were you noticing about the students? How were the students responding?
3. Were you thinking of any alternative strategies at that time?
4. Did any student reactions cause you to act differently than you had planned?

This strategy was used with twelve experienced teachers.

Peterson and Clark found, not surprisingly, that teachers generally followed a certain pattern. As they taught, if student behavior fell within certain preestablished guidelines, teachers continued with their plans. Occasionally, teachers deviated from this pattern when student feedback indicated that it was time to move to another alternative.

Peterson and Clark developed a model to explain teacher's intractive decisions and postulated that teachers generally followed one of four paths during their teaching. Path 1 is the path described above: teachers teaching from the plan all the way through the lesson. Path 2 is when teachers decide during a lesson that things aren't going very smoothly but they are unable to think of an alternative, so they move on through the plan. Path 3 is when a teacher knows student behavior is out of bounds, tries an alternative plan, but the alternative plan doesn't work either. In Path 4, teachers know there is a problem with student behavior so they try a new teaching behavior which works. This behavior becomes a new activity that the teacher will eventually develop into a routine. The process amounts to something of a thoughtful trial and error procedure.

Findings of their research which compared teacher decision making with student achievement were instructive. They found that student achievement in abstract thinking was correlated with classrooms where teachers changed instruction in response to student behavior (path 4). On the other hand, there was a negative correlation between Path 4 teachers and student achievement, suggesting that Path 4 teachers influenced abstract, higher order thinking skills, while Path 1 teachers enhanced factual, low lever kinds of thinking. This model was helpful in that it allowed researchers to compare teacher's interactive decisions with different kinds of student achievement.

Shavelson and Stern (1981), building on the work by Joyce (1978-79), Peterson & Clark (1978), Shavelson (1976), and Snow (1972), developed an expanded version of the model described above. This model includes two new paths. One path allows for the teacher to ask herself while teaching, "Is immediate action necessary or is delayed action necessary?" If delayed action is necessary, the teacher then must remember to take delayed action and store information for the future. This model extends the Peterson and Clark (1978) model but it is not without its critics.

Peterson and Clark (1984), after reviewing the research on teacher interactive decision making, have suggested that the models described above are insufficient. These models assume that student behavior is the only antecedent to teacher decision making. Certainly, there are other thoughts and beliefs that teachers hold which affect their decision making. A consideration of those thoughts and beliefs follows.

Teacher's Implicit Theories and Beliefs

Research in the area of teacher beliefs and theories is concerned with the frames of references through which teachers perceive and process information. There is a paucity of research in the area; however, a study conducted by Elbaz (1983) provides a good example of this body of research.

Elbaz (1983) conducted a study of one high school English teacher (Sarah) and found that Sarah's implicit theories and beliefs were based on her practical knowledge. Elbaz suggests that, "theory is seen (by Sarah) as something broad, general, comprehensive" (p. 102-103) and notes that it seems to set limits on Sarah's teaching. Sarah tended to reify such terms as thinking and learning, feeling as if there is certain all encompassing knowledge on the subject that only experts are privy to. When Sarah and her colleagues developed a course called, The Learning Course, they were set up for failure because they felt as if their practical knowledge was somehow inferior to knowledge developed by "experts."

This kind of thinking seems to be related to the Rational Ends-Means Model of curriculum discussed earlier in this article. Teachers are trained to believe that there is one best way to teach and that researchers are searching constantly for that one best way. Moreover, the refinements to this body of research are so frequent and, sometimes contradictory, that teachers believe only a professional who studies it full time can hope to understand it. Many teachers spend the first few years of their teaching, especially the first year, wondering what the ideal way to teach a particular lesson is and feeling guilty that they are not meeting some ideal perceived "standard." This belief leads to a lack of confidence and an overreliance on "expert opinion." Ultimately, unless teachers are encouraged to trust their planning, thinking and decision making processes, they will seek fool-proof activities — the cookbook approach to teaching that is so ineffective.

Implications for the Practitioner

What this research suggests is that it is possible to be "overplanned," and that such specific planning may act to the detriment of effective teaching. More specifically, very detailed lesson plans may be simply executed without regard for the need to adjust instruction from moment to moment based on the way students are responding to it.

Curriculum planning, in view of the research on teacher thinking, can also result in too much specificity. A curriculum guide that specifies goals, objectives, content and instructional procedures may be viewed by teachers as too restrictive and can be easily ignored. Unfortunately, if a teacher rejects the instructional approaches because of their rigidity, the accompanying goals may be lost as well.

What does this research suggest about teaching and teacher education? First, teachers should be encouraged to trust their own judgments about what kind of instructional treatments students require at any given time. Lock-step approaches to teaching should be avoided. Second, teachers should be skilled in reading student teaching and adjusting their teaching, quickly, on the basis of that feedback. Further, they must be encouraged to evaluate each approach they use and reflect thoughtfully on *their* performance each day. Finally, teachers must have the opportunity to discuss *their* teaching with other professionals in a non-evaluative setting. This means that groups of teachers should meet for the expressed purpose of talking about *their* context with *their* students. The reinforcement and encouragement of fellow professionals will contribute much to the teacher's self-confidence and willingness to modify instructional approaches as needed in the classroom.

REFERENCES

Clark, C. (1983). Research on teacher planning: An inventory of the knowledge base. In David C. Smith (Ed.), *Essential knowledge for beginning educators*. Washington, D.C.: American Association of Colleges for Teacher Education.

Clark, C. & Peterson, P. (1984). *Teacher's thought processes*. (Occasional Paper No. 72). East Lansing, MI: Institute for Research on Teaching, Michigan State University.

Clark, C. & Yinger, R. (1977). Research on teacher thinking. *Curriculum Inquiry, 7*, 279-304.

Elbaz, F. (1983). *Teacher thinking: A study of practical knowledge*. New York: Nichols Publishing Company.

Eisner, E.W. (1967). Educational objectives: Help or hindrance? *School Review, 75*, 250-260.

Gage, N. (1963). Paradigms for research on teaching. In N. Gage (Ed.) *Handbook of research on teaching*. Chicago: Rand McNally.

Joyce, B. (1978-79). Toward a theory of information processing in teaching. *Educational Research Quarterly, 3* (4), 66-77

Macdonald, J. (1965). Myths about instruction. *Educational Leadership, 22*, (8), 571-576, 609-617.

Macdonald, J., Wolfson, B. & Zaret, E. (1973). *Reschooling society: A conceptual model*. Washington, D.C.: Association for Supervision and Curriculum Development.

Peterson, P. & Clark, C. (1978). Teacher's reports of their cognitive processes during teaching. *American Educational Research Journal, 15*, 555-565.

Popham, J. & Baker, E. (1970). *Systematic instruction*. Englewood Cliffs, NJ: Prentice-Hall.

Shavelson, R. (1976). Teacher's decision making. In N.L. Gage (Ed.), *The psychology of teaching methods* (Yearbook of the National Society for the Study of Education). Chicago: University of Chicago Press.

Shavelson, R. & Stern, P. (1981). Research on teacher's pedagogical thoughts, judgments, decisions and behavior. *Review of Educational Research, 51*, 455-498.

Snow, R. (1972). *A model teaching training system: An overview*. (Research and Development Memorandum No. 92). Stanford Center for Research and Development in Teaching, School of Education, Stanford University. (ERIC Reproduction Service No. Ed 437.)

Taba, H. (1962). *Curriculum development, theory and practice*. New York: Harcourt, Brace & World.

Tyler, R. (1950). *Basic principles of curriculum and instruction*. Illinois: University of Chicago Press.

Yinger, R. (1979). Routines in teacher planning. *Theory Into Practice, 18*, 163-169.

Zahorik, J. (1975). Teacher's planning models. *Educational Leadership, 33*, 134-139.

February, 1985

6. About Teacher Stress*

Stress is a killer. All of us have been warned of the awful effects that too much stress can have on our physical and mental health, our careers, and our relations with other people. Unrelieved stress has been associated with increases in heart disease, stroke, psychic disorders, child abuse, criminal violence, divorce, alcohol and drug abuse and a plethora of other modern ills. Obviously, we cannot expect education professionals to be immune from the stresses of modern life, but it appears as if educators, as a group, suffer from rather distinct and unique forms of stress, and that the amount of stress they encounter is greater than that of many other occupational groups. In fact, upon completing a survey of literature on the subject, Samples (1976) was led to state, "schools comprise some of the highest stress ecologies in our society."

Stress has been defined in various ways, ranging from fairly general definitions to quite specific ones. Selye (1956) defined stress as any non-specific response of the body to any demand made upon it. Typically, stress results when an individual's equilibrium is upset — when our "behavior modes are not adequate to meet the demands of situations and when the failure to adapt has serious consequences." (Needle, Griffin, Svendsen, 1981). Occupational stress occurs when a discrepancy arises between the worker's values, needs and expectations and a work environment which has restricted rewards and job demands and requirements exceeding the resources of the worker. (Levi, 1979; Needle, Griffin, Svendesen, 1980).

Our physiological reactions to stress are called the General Adaptation Syndrome (GAS), a term proposed by Selye (1956). The GAS is comprised of three stages: alarm, where the body is charged with secretions of the adrenal glands, preparing it for "flight or fight"; resistance, during which the spleen, thymus and lymphatic systems shrink and resistance to disease is thus lowered; and exhaustion, in which all adaptive energy is expended and the organism feels depleted. Apparently it is the excessive repetition of this biological drama that causes other physiological disorders such as hypertension and fatigue.

Beyond these physical effects, too much stress may lower job satisfaction (Selye, 1974; Pelletier, 1977), impair thinking and problem-solving, and generally reduce our capacity to cope with our environment. (Sparks, 1979). It appears, though, that not all of the effects of stress are negative. Some writers argue that some stress is needed simply to motivate any action at all; in other words, the organism must be slightly out of equilibrium in order to be motivated to restore the desired balance. Friedman (1980) says that "teaching as a profession demands both physical and mental alertness that can be energized by good stress (eustress) and debilitated by bad stress (distress)." Following this argument, instead of attempting to remove all stress from the workplace, effort should be concentrated on helping teachers cope effectively with distress and capitalize on eustress.

Other researchers present a much more gloomy view of stress and its effects on teachers. In a 1977 survey of its readers, *Instructor* magazine found that 75% of the 9000 responders reported that teacher absence is frequently stress-related. Dedrick and his colleagues (1981) reported that among the Iowa teachers they

**Larry C. Holt shared in preparing this column*

surveyed, 57% had given serious thought to a career change — with the number reaching 72% for high school teachers.

Cichon et al. (1978) found that over half of the teachers in his sample reported physical illnesses believed to be related to job stress. In another study, chronic physical maladies were reported by 45% of the teachers surveyed, all of whom believed that they resulted, at least in part, from occupational stress. Among these chronic complaints were high blood pressure (12%), kidney and bladder trouble (11%), arthritis (7%), breathing problems (6%), insomnia (3.8%), gastritis (4.1%), ulcer (4%), anemia (3.6%), asthma (3.4%), colitis (3.2%) and heart disease (2.3%). (Needle, Griffin, Svendsen, 1981).

Other symptoms of stress were reported by almost 96% of the respondents in the same study. These included the most frequently cited, "feeling completely worn out at the end of the day," followed closely by difficulty in getting up in the morning. Teachers who reported the highest stress levels also reported a significantly higher incidence of symptom presence as well.

In its advanced stages, Friedman points out (1980), stress may result in "burnout," a condition which produces cynical and negative attitudes toward students, depression and decreased productivity (Abels, 1978; Scott, 1980; Spaniol, 1979). Not only does burnout reduce the effectiveness of instruction children receive, it also results in the loss of able teachers who simply leave the profession (Scott, 1980). Younger teachers who still feel they have career mobility are the most likely to leave the profession, taking with them some of the restorative effect every profession receives as a benefit from its newest members (Brackman, 1980). In New York State, the average age of teachers has increased from 34 to 38 in just 5 years, and Connecticut's average teacher age jumped 3.7 years, from 35.1 to 38.9, in just two years (Cerra, 1980). Both of these figures indicate that there are few new people entering the profession and that the youngest members are leaving it; neither condition bodes well for our system of public education.

Finally, stress seems to manifest itself in growing numbers of early retirements and retirements for disability. In 1979 in New York State, 51 of 149 disability retirements among teachers were for psychiatric or neurological conditions, a figure said to be a "drastic increase" over previous years (Maletta, 1980).

Sources of Stress in Teaching

What are the sources of this debilitating stress for teachers? Apparently, three categories of stress (Pettegrew and Wolf, 1982) account for most of the varieties teachers encounter: role-related stress (Kahn, 1970), task-based stress (Tung and Koch, 1980), and environmental stress (Pettegrew, et al., 1981).

Task and work event stress, or those which are associated with specific tasks the teacher must perform in the teaching role, provide one of the clearest sets of "stressors," objects or events which produce stress. Using a "life events" inventory, Cichon and Koff (1978) found that the most stressful events for teachers included involuntary transfer, dealing with student disruptions, unfavorable evaluation by supervisors and physical threats by students. A similar survey by the American Federation of Teachers (1981) showed inordinate time demands, disruptive students, lack of administrative support (called "incompetent administrators" in a United Teachers of New York study conducted in 1980), lack of parental support and looming budget cuts as the most stress-producing events. Olander and Farrell (1979) found that teachers were often frustrated by lack of time for individual work, working without a preparation period and finding additional resources for instruction, all of which produced moderate to severe amounts of stress. Wilson's (1980) study reveals time management, interpersonal conflict, and parent/student relationships as significant stress producers, while Derrick (et al., 1981) supplements this listing with student apathy, non-teaching duties, financial pressures, lack of community support and positive feedback from administrators, multi-ability students, lack of recognition, lack of input into significant decisions and lack of colleague support.

Stress also results from the expectations associated with the teaching role, role-related stressors. Kahn (1964) describes the phenomenon as the discrepancy between what individuals expect from a role and their actual experiences in the role. In this way, role-related stress is tied most closely to management practices which permit an individual to reconcile his or her expectations with the actual work situation and the achievement of a good "personal-environmental fit" in the workplace. (Pettegrew and Wolf, 1982). As a example, teachers who are orderly in their personal habits, and expect schools to be orderly places, are likely to be frustrated by the sometimes barely contained exuberance of an open-space or unstructured school setting. What is worse is when the teacher feels that he or she has no control over the discrepancy, as when those of us raised to think that teaching is a respectable and dignified career witness undignified behavior by some of our colleagues or hear comments in the community about teachers' ineffectiveness and sloth.

Although there are not many studies about role-related stress and teaching, this type of stress appears to be particularly harmful. Tosi and Tosi (1970) found that role conflict and role ambiguity both have significant relationships with high teacher turnover rates, with teachers who experience a great deal of conflict between their expectations and perceived occupational reality and those who are unsure of the proper role they are to play being more likely to abandon the profession. Similarly, Aaron (1976) linked role conflict and role ambiguity to absenteeism among teachers. Finally, it appears as if the current emphasis on accountability serves to produce role conflict - and subsequent stress - on teachers. Quite suddenly, teachers as a group are being held responsible for a host of problems displayed by schools, students, American business and industry and the society at large (Derrick, et al., 1981). Whereas teachers were once viewed as guardians of our intellectual heritage and the mentors of our children, they now find the profession under assault for ineptness, incompetence, and cynicism. The resulting role conflict appears to be profound and, in many cases, disabling.

In categorizing stressors, Needle and his colleagues (1981) were able to provide categories of stress producers that summarize much of the foregoing material. Their eight categories contain a number of specific indicators which are important for administrators working to remove sources of teacher stress. These are: non-teaching problems, such as overcrowded classrooms, contract negotiations and lack of public support; time demands such as overwork, lack of planning time, demands of exceptional students; student problems related to drug abuse, apathy and vandalism; lack of flexibility in schedule as indicated by an inability to leave the classroom for "a breather." or the difficulty of taking a day off and still "covering" classes; behavior problems and talking with parents about them;

involuntary transfer; threats, whether of unsatisfactory evaluations or actual physical harm; and the amount of control exercised over individual teacher initiatives by district policy or administrative censorship. In short, the most stressful situations are ones over which teachers feel they have little control, ones in which they feel that they cannot devote enough time to instruction, and ones which highlight the intrinsic conflict between the need to manage behavior problems and the real objectives of the class session.

Somewhat ironically, administrators, often cited as major stress factors for teachers, share many of the same stressors with their teaching colleagues. Koff (et al., 1981) found that the top stressors for administrators were forcing the resignation or dismissal of a teacher, dealing with unsatisfactory performance by professional staff, involuntary transfer to another principalship, preparing for a strike, teacher refusal to follow policies, criticism in the press, the last week of school year, forced staff reduction, legal action against the school, and assault upon a staff member. Gmelch and Swent (1981) add time management, staff evaluation, resolving conflicts with parents, and gaining public approval to produce a list that complements the stress factors for teachers almost perfectly! Koff (et al., 1981) concludes that events dealing with conflict between administrators and staff were most stressful, followed by events which threatened job, physical, and fiscal security. Relatively low amounts of stress are produced by routine, expected and accepted duties, such as hiring new staff, managing policies, and working with central office staff.

Coping with Stress

While all of this sounds uncompromisingly negative, there is some good research news regarding stress management and coping behavior. To understand the research message, though, it is necessary to return to a theoretical model of stress response which gives insight to the nature of stress control intervention. Kahn (1970) summarizes the stress response into four stages: perception of the demand or stressor, labeling of the perception, physiological, psychological and/or behavioral response to the stressor, and reception of the consequences of the response. Clearly, the likelihood of stress is increased when an individual sees an actual or anticipated threat as being beyond his or her ability to cope with it. In other words, it is largely the individual's "perception and assessment of the environment which labels the situation as negative or positive resulting in physical as well as mental reaction." (Friedman, 1980). Thus, to a large degree, we can control stress, and probably do so more effectively than we can remove stress producers from our environment.

Predictably, people with an internal locus of control tend to have more control over personal stress than do "externals," primarily because they see themselves, in general, as being more in control of their environments (Friedman, 1980). In addition, individuals must believe, and in fact expect, that training in stress control is going to be successful, and that this conviction is a necessary prerequisite to even the most preliminary attempts at coping with stress (Friedman, 1980).

Among the most useful coping strategies are cognitive restructuring (Rose, 1977) or cognitive behavior modification (Meichenbaum, 1977). These strategies consist of challenging irrational beliefs, changing self-talk and role rehearsal.

Perhaps the simplest of these strategies, at least conceptually, is challenging irrational beliefs. In essence, the individual disputes and rejects irrational beliefs and self-defeating thoughts and replaces them with self-assuring statements (Friedman, 1980). Changing self-talk is where the teachers change what they "say" about themselves in given situations from negative and deprecating statements to positive and encouraging ones. In both of these forms of cognitive coping, it is important for colleagues to provide each other with opportunities to challenge their own irrational beliefs about themselves and see evidence of their self-worth and adequacy. Another strategy, cognitive role rehearsal, (Janis, 1971) is used to give teachers a chance to predict how they might act in a stressful situation and visualize themselves coping successfully with it.

Other strategies listed by Needle (et al., 1981) are used with varying degrees of effectiveness. Positive comparisons help control the meaning of a problem by getting teachers to perceive that things are better now than they were a year ago and that they will be even better next year. Another method is positive action, where teachers search for positive aspects of the job, and a third is substitution of rewards, in which individuals are encouraged to maximize the desirability of the positive aspects of the work and minimize the negative aspects. Among the most common responses is selectively ignoring problems and focusing on the most gratifying aspects of teaching.

Because many teachers have "caretaker" personalities, they tend to think of others before attending to their own needs. They need to learn to "take" sometimes just in order to replenish the storehouse from which they are expected to give (Wangberg, 1982). Much can also be accomplished by teaching teachers the techniques for systematic and progressive relaxation, whether meditation or some less formal method.

Stress is taking a heavy toll on our teachers and is, in turn, affecting our schools and our children. However, stress can be managed and controlled. Attention should be given to reducing the in-school variables that produce stress and to training teachers for individual stress management. Just as teachers are prepared through inservice education for other conditions that are part of the educational setting (such as mainstreaming, bilingual education and competency testing) proper emphasis must be placed on training them to cope with the unique and widespread stresses associated with their careers in contemporary education.

REFERENCES

Aaron, D.S. Social-psychological correlates of teacher absenteeism, Unpublished Doctoral Dissertation, Ohio State University, 1976.

Abels, P. The psychologically battered helpers: what do helpers do with client-triggered stress? Battered Person Workshop Paper, Case Western Reserve University, 1978.

Brockman, F. interview in Older teachers confront stress in changed era, New York *Times*, October 14, 1980.

Cascio, C. Careers: teachers under duress, Washington *Post*, June 11, 1981.

Cerra, F. Older teachers confront stress in changed era, New York *Times*, October 14, 1980.

Cichon, D., R. Koff, Teaching events stress inventory, paper presented at American Education Research Association convention, Toronto, 1978.

Derrick, C.V., R.R. Hawkes and J.K. Smith Teacher stress: a descriptive study of concerns," N.A.S.S.P. *Bulletin*, 65: 31-35, December, 1981.

Friedman, G. Relationship between teachers' locus of control and the effectiveness of directed versus self-directed stress reduction, unpublished doctoral dissertation, University of Cincinnati, 1980.

Gmelch, W.H. and B. Swent. Stress in the principalship, N.A.S.S.P. *Bulletin*, 65:16-19, December, 1981.

Janis, I. *Stress and Frustration*, New York: Harcourt, Brace, and Jovanovich, 1971.

Kahn, R.L., D.M. Wolfe and R.P. Quinn, et al., *Organizational Stress*, New York, John Wiley, 1964.

Kahn, R.L. Some propositions toward a researchable conceptualization of stress, in J.W. McGrath (ed.) *Social and Psychological Factors in Stress*, New York: Holt, Rinehart and Winston, 1970.

Koff, R., J.M. Laffey, G.E. Olson and D.J. Cichon, Executive stress and the school administrator, N.A.S.S.P. *Bulletin*, 65:1-9, December, 1981.

Levi, L. Occupational mental health, *JOM* 21:26-31, 1979.

Maletta, N., Interview in the New York *Times*, October 14, 1980.

Meichenbaum, D. *Cognitive Behavior Modification*, Morristown, N.J.: General Learning Press, 1977.

Needle, R.T. Griffin, R. Svendsen. Teacher stress: sources and consequences, *Journal of School Health*, 50:96-99, 1980.

Needle, R., T. Griffin and R. Svendsen. Occupational stress, *Journal of School Health*, 51:175-181, March 1981.

Olander, H.T. and M. Farrell. Professional problems of elementary teachers, *Journal of Teacher Education*, 21:276-280, 1979.

Pelletier, K.R. *Mind As Healer, Mind As Slayer*, New York: Delta, 1977.

Pettegrew, L.S., et al., Effects of job-related stress on medical center employee communication style, *Journal of Occupational Behavior*, 2:235-253, 1981.

Rose, S.D. *Group Therapy, A Behavioral Approach*, Englewood Cliffs: Prentice-Hall, 1977.

Samples, B. Sanity in the classroom, *Science Teacher*, 43: 24-27, 1976.

Scott, J.D. Why teachers quit, *Cincinnati* Magazine, 13:44-49, 1980.

Selye, H. *The Stress of Life*, New York: McGraw-Hill, 1956.

Spaniol, A. Teacher burnout, *Instructor*, 88P56-62, 1979.

Sparks, D. Teacher burnout: a teacher center tackles the issue, *Today's Education*, 68:37-39, November/December, 1979.

Tosi, D.J. and H. Tosi. Some correlates of role ambiguity among public school teachers, *Journal of Human Relations*, 18:1068-1076, 1970.

Tung, R.L. and J. Koch, School administrators: sources of stress and ways of coping with it, in Cooper and Marshall (eds.) *White Collar and Professional Stress*, Chichester, England: John Wiley, 1980.

Wangburg, E. Helping teachers cope with stress, *Educational Leadership*, 452-454, March 1982.

Wilson, C.F. Stress profiles for teachers, San Diego; Department of Education, San Diego County California, 1980.

Wolf, G.E. Validating measures of teacher stress, *American Educational Research Journal*, 198:373-396, 1982.

November, 1982

7. Promotion and Retention*

Some questions just will not go away. Whether students should be retained in a grade or promoted to the next one is one of those questions that has plagued educators for most of this century. Who gets promoted or retained? What criteria are used to decide? What are the effects of those decisions on the student's school performance, personal adjustment and social relationships? Even without satisfactory answers, educators must act every spring to promote or retain individual students. The decision to retain a student is not made lightly, nor is it made with relish. The anguish of the teachers and administrators, though, is probably only a portion of that experienced by the student and his or her family.

For the purpose of this column, grade retention is defined as requiring a student who has been in a given grade level for a full school year to remain at that level for a subsequent school year (Jackson, 1975). Retention should not be confused with the practice of successfully keeping potential drop-outs enrolled in school, a practice sometimes referred to as "retaining" them. As used here, the term "retention" is synonymous with all of those antique terms that struck terror into our own hearts as school children: being "left back," "failing," or "flunking." It is used in preference to the more awkward (and sometimes confusing) term, "nonpromotion."

For the most part, this article does not deal with the practice of retaining a student in a single subject or two. Instead, we have chosen to focus on the repeating of an entire grade — a practice which is quite widespread in the United States.

Retention is not a new practice. Retention rates for students in British schools were very high as early as the late 16th century (Hess, 1978). By the early 19th century in the United States, grade retention was the preferred method for dealing with learning deficiencies (Cunningham and Owens, 1976). And by the end of the 19th century, the practice was so common that nearly every other child was retained at least once during his or her school career (Larson, 1955). It was in the 1930's, with the rise of Progressive Education, that educators began to question the practice because of its potentially adverse effects on social and emotional development. Instead of repeating a grade, most students were passed on to the next grade where they were grouped by ability and given special help. Thus, simultaneously, the practice of social promotion and tracking by ability became popular in the public schools (Rose, et al., 1983).

Now, promotion and retention decisions are made on the basis of four common criteria: (1) student's current achievement level; (2) personal and home factors such as age, social maturity, physical development, and parental attitudes; (3) what is in "the best interest" of the student; and (4) the number of times the student has been retained before (Rose, et al., 1983). Most often, the principal makes the final decision, although he or she is usually assisted by teachers and a counselor or school psychologist.

In the past ten years, retention rates for students have increased somewhat over the 1970's. At present, retention rates at the middle level range from less than 2% to about 13% of the school's population. Some of this variability is regional, but most seems to be a function of population density and the presence of large

Eunice Mims assisted in the development of this column.

minority populations. It remains most disturbing that retention rates for minority students are nearly three to four times as high as those for majority students (Jackson, 1975). Children were most likely to be enrolled below the grade level of their age-mates if "(a) they were black or of Spanish origin, (b) their families were below the poverty level, (c) the head of household had less than twelve years of education, and (d) they lived in the southeastern region of the United States." (Rose, et al., 1983).

This issue of retention is especially important at the middle level because the trends in retention rates by grade level show that, while the highest rates occur in the primary years (grade 1, in particular) they decline throughout elementary school and increase sharply at the 7th grade, peaking at 10th. This suggests that the middle level school imposes somewhat more stringent promotion standards than the intermediate grades, and that the student's first major exposure to a subject-oriented curriculum taught by a number of subject-matter specialist teachers may affect school performance.

Unfortunately, the research on grade retention is not of uniformly high quality. Therefore, it is difficult to draw unassailable conclusions about it.

After reviewing forty-nine studies that represented nearly the entire corpus of research on the subject, Jackson (1975) said that most of the studies were biased in some way or another toward a predetermined conclusion. Studies which compare retained students with promoted students are biased toward indicating that promotion is more beneficial because it compares retained students who were having difficulties with promoted students whose difficulties were not as severe, as evidenced by the fact that they were promoted. Even matching students on the basis of age, grade level, IQ and academic grades may not be adequate, he says, because there is no assurance that the comparisons are made "among pupils experiencing similar difficulties as relevant to grade retention." (Jackson, 1975).

The second type of study compares the condition of retained students after promotion with their condition prior to promotion, a design which is biased toward indicating that pupils benefit from retention. This bias is introduced because any development the student experiences is attributed to being retained in the grade. What isn't known in this case is if the progress results only from the passage of time and would have been the same if the student had progressed with his classmates.

In the third type of study, students with difficulties were randomly assigned either to a promoted group or to a retained group. While this design eliminates most experimental bias, it raises certain ethical and professional issues about the treatment of subjects and potentially harmful effects on the child's subsequent school career. For this reason, only three such studies were reported, all conducted between 1929 and 1941. And while the design was superior, wisdom dictates against forming broad generalizations about modern schools from three studies that were conducted half a century ago.

Despite all of the limitations, Jackson is confident enough in the trends indicated by his review to come to the following conclusion: "neither the few soundly designed studies nor the major portion of the inadequately designed studies suggest that grade retention is more beneficial for pupils having difficulties in school than is promotion to the subsequent grade." (Jackson, 1975: 614). He continues, "the results of the few experimental design analyses suggest that grade retention is no more productive than grade promotion..." and that when all of the results are taken as a whole: "there is no reliable body of evidence to indicate that grade retention is more beneficial than grade promotion for students with serious academic or adjustment difficulties." (Jackson, 1975:627).

If there is something to be learned from Jackson's general conclusions, a look at more detailed findings of these studies and others conducted since 1975 will also be instructive. Generally, these studies divide into two groups: those dealing with the academic effects of student retention and those which investigate personal adjustment and social development as a function of retention or promotion. The remainder of this article is organized in the same fashion.

Academic Effects

Ostensibly, retention is designed to affect the students' academic performance. Repeating a grade will expose them to information and skills missed on the first time through, allow them time to develop more mature study skills and habits, and give them the opportunity to succeed at tasks more appropriate to their level. How does this work in practice? The research evidence, while mixed, suggests that it doesn't work very well unless fairly specific conditions are met.

In an early study, Coffield and Blommers (1954) studied the academic performance of 147 Iowa school children who had been retained at least one time between grades 3 and 7. When performance in grade 7 was studied, the researchers were able to conclude that:

(1) failed pupils gained only six months in Iowa Test of Basic Skills scores during the repeat year and still failed to achieve the grade level norm; they tended to gain approximately one year and three months during the two years following failure;
(2) the educational progress of failed students during the two years following failure is not any greater than promoted students (matched with the retained students) who spent only one year in the next highest grade; and
(3) the educational progress of seventh grade pupils who have been retained once is on a par with that of matched, promoted students who have spent one year less in school.

In short, there appears to be no advantage to keeping a child in a grade for one additional year. In the words of the authors, "if the consideration is solely a matter of educational achievement, it does seem clear that little is gained by requiring the repetition of a grade." (Coffield and Blommers, 1956:249).

It is clear from these findings, though, that if retention is to occur, it should be done early rather than later in the child's school career. The greatest differences in 7th grade achievement gains between retained and promoted students occurred when the retention occurred in the 5th or 6th grade rather than in the 3rd or 4th. Similar findings were reported by McAfee (1981) who concluded that the more beneficial effects of early retention come from the fact that retention decisions in the early grades tend to be made on the basis of variables besides academic achievement alone. Often, a child's size, social maturity, and connections with class peers will enter such a decision, along with the wishes of the parents. Such a balanced review, he argues, may be the key to determining whether or not retention will benefit an individual student or not.

The strongest criticism of retention for academic reasons comes from Kamii and Weikart (1963). Examining the grades, IQ scores and achievement scores of 7th graders who had been retained, they concluded that grades may be assigned to retained pupils on the basis of criteria other than ability and achievement. In fact, fifty-seven percent of the retained pupils' grades were D's or F's, compared with the promoted students, fifty-five percent of whom were awarded A's and B's. Approximately one-third of each group received C's, but no retained students received A's and fewer than 10% earned a B; among promoted students, there were no F's and approximately 10% earned D's.

On achievement measures, Kamii and Weikart found that the retained group, on the whole, achieved less in seven years than the promoted group achieved in six. Further, IQ scores showed that the retained group had a mean IQ of 94 while the promoted group had an average of 112.6.

What is most important, though, is the relationship among these measures. According to the researchers, low IQ's do not adequately account for all of the D and F grades given to the retained group. Even given the same IQ range, "regularly promoted pupils get better marks than the ones who have been retained. The lower IQ's of the retained pupils do not account very well for their poor marks" (Kamii and Weikart, 1963:457).

If IQ seems to offer an inadequate explanation, perhaps achievement and the mastery of basic skills does. Social studies and English, they hypothesized, depend heavily upon reading skills. Thus, one would expect that students with lower reading ability would do poorly in these subjects. It didn't work exactly that way. "The retained group did not make a single B or A in these subjects, whereas the A's and B's earned by the normal reading group were spread over almost its entire range of reading skills. Also, given the same ability in reading, the regularly promoted pupils consistently earned better marks in these two subjects." (Kamii and Weikart, 1963:457). If the differences in grades cannot be attributed to IQ or to achievement ability, it must be a function of the criteria used to award grades. The authors' research suggests that retained students are routinely given lower grades, perhaps accounting for diminished motivation and achievement orientation.

Elligett and Tocco (1983) argue just as forcefully, though, for the beneficial effects of grade retention. After studying the effects of the Pinellas County (Florida) grade retention policy, they found that the "academic performance of retained students...had substantially improved between the year prior to retention and the year following promotion" to the next grade. (p. 734). In fact, they found that students "who had been retained in grade 4 scored eight months above the fifth-grade national norms when they completed grade 5." (p. 735). Similar median improvement gains are cited for students in grades 6 through 8 as well.

On the basis of these findings, the researchers conclude "when students were promoted after a year of retention, their achievement in the grade to which they were promoted showed substantial improvement over their achievement prior to retention occurred despite the increased difficulty of the curricula and tests and the higher level of the norms in the grades to which these students had been promoted." (p. 735).

Why are these findings so different from the others? Evidently, it can be attributed to two factors. First, the achievement measures were gathered from a competency-based test. In other words, the curriculum was geared to the accomplishment of a specified number of very specific objectives that were keyed to a measurement instrument. Thus, if the student spend a second year working on the same, carefully specified, objectives, chances are good he will develop additional mastery. Second, placement was determined after consideration of the student's total school record. Therefore, other variables were considered which resulted in the promotion of some students who did not score above the minimum competency level. In most cases, the parents supported the decision to retain or promote the pupil, so some measure of parental support and at-home intervention might also be assumed.

Holmes and Matthews (1983), however, remain unconvinced of the benefits of retention. Upon completing a metanalysis of 44 major studies of retention and promotion, they concluded "that nonpromotion had a negative effect on the pupils..." particularly in the areas of language arts, reading and work-study skills.

But retention decisions are most often criticized for their effects on the personal and social adjustment of the child. The extent to which those criticisms are grounded in reality in addressed next.

Personal-Social Adjustment Effects

Holmes and Matthews (1983) are just as convinced of the harmful effects of retention on the student's adjustment as they are that it is harmful to future academic achievement. They reported that the retained students scored nearly one-third of a standard deviation below promoted peers in social adjustment, emotional adjustment and behavior. Furthermore, they had considerably lower self-concepts and were less favorably disposed toward school. It is on the basis of this analysis that they conclude, "the potential for negative effects consistently outweighs positive outcomes."

Early research by Walter Cook (1941) suggested that schools with lower ratios of over-age pupils (students who were retained and who are older than their classmates) tended to adjust instruction to the ability of the child more thoroughly than schools with higher ratios of retention. In other words, teachers in low retention rate schools seem to do a better job of individualizing instruction.

The extent to which over-age pupils are accepted by their classmates is an issue as well. Upon conducting a sociometric study of the extent to which over-age pupils were accepted by classmates, Morrison and Perry (1956) concluded that "it seemed clear that these over-age children were not well accepted by their peers in the class groups studied...it would seem that wide disparity in age from the median of the group was a factor which limited opportunity for choice status." (p. 219). They went on to report that "a total of ninety percent of these over-age children were found below the medians of their respective class groups in sociometric status." Things are not quite so bleak at the 7th and 8th grade as in the 4th, 5th and 6th, though. At the higher grade level, athletic prowess and other forms of sophistication demonstrated by over-age students seem to have an important role in their acceptance by classmates, particularly with the opposite sex. Because of the need for status in the group, particularly at the middle level, the authors express concern that over-age students may seek inappropriate recognition from their peers because they have been denied academic recognition by their teachers and the school.

It is best not to leap to a lot of conclusions about adjustment, though. As early as 1941 Rudolph Anfinson found that the incidence of adjustment problems was no higher among retained students than among promoted students. In fact, both groups showed the full range of student adjustment to school, from extremely well-adjusted to extremely poorly adjusted.

Some things can be said about the effects of promotion and non-promotion on students, and these are best summarized by Purkerson and Whitfield (1981). "Not being promoted does affect personality development, but not to the point of being the primary cause of future maladjustment. The acceptance of non-promoted students by their classmates is severe in grades five and six, but much less severe in grades seven and eight. Finally, as a rule, if nonpromotion is to occur, the earlier the better. Further, self-concept and achievement do not exist separately and apart from academic achievement. Very simply, some low achieving students benefit from non-promotion; some do not. The educator's task is to do everything possible to make correct decisions."

Does retention help students? Some students may be helped sometimes by retention, but the general conclusion seems to be that the practice is not encouraged by the long history of research on the topic. Most importantly, though, it is clear that simply repeating the same treatment, unless it is connected to very specific learning objectives, is not likely to do much good. The question to retain, then, becomes two-fold: "Shall we retain , and, if we do, what will we all do differently this time?"

REFERENCES

Afinson, Rudolph (1941). School progress and pupil adjustment, *Elementary School Journal*, 41: 507-514.

Coffield, W.H. and P. Blommers (1956). Effects on non promotion on educational achievement in the elementary school, *Journal of Educational Psychology*, 47:235-250.

Cook, Walter (1941). Some effects of the maintenance of high standards of promotion, *Elementary School Journal*, 41:430-437

Cunningham, W.G. and R. Owens (1976). Social promotion: problem or solution? *NASSP Bulletin*, 60:25-29.

Elligett, J.K. and T.S. Tocco (1983) The promotion-retention policy in Pinellas County, Florida, *Phi Delta Kappan*, 64: 733-735.

Hess, F. (1978). Issues in education: a documented look at seven current topics, ERIC ED 158, 391.

Holmes, C.T. and K.M. Matthews (1983). The effects of nonpromotion on elementary and junior high pupils: a meta-analysis, ERIC ED 229, 876

Jackson, G.G. (1975). The research evidence on the effects of grade retention, *Review of Educational Research*, 45: 613-635.

Kamii, C.K., and D.P. Weikart (1963). Marks, achievement and intelligence of seventh graders who were retained once in elementary school, *Journal of Educational Research*, 56: 452-459.

Larson, R.E. (1955). Age-grade status of Iowa elementary school pupils, unpublished doctoral dissertation, Iowa State University.

McAfee, Jackson K. (1981). Toward a theory of promotion: does retaining students really work? ERIC, ED 204, 871.

Morrison, I. and I. Perry (1956). Acceptance of over-age children by their class-mates, *Elementary School Journal* 56: 217-220.

Purkerson, R. and E. Whitfield (1981). Failure syndrome: stress factor for middle school children, ERIC ED 207, 680.

Rose, J.S., F.J. Medway, V.L. Cantrell, and S.H. Marus (1983). A fresh look at the retention-promotion controversy, *Journal of School Psychology*, 21:201-211.

November, 1985

II
Teaching Middle School Students

1. Motivating Students

By the time students enter the middle school, interest in exploring and learning, which seemed to be intrinsic when they entered first grade, has declined appreciably (3,10). Middle school teachers frequently cite the lack of motivation as a primary cause of students' failure to learn. This column will review the findings of motivation theory and research and recommend ways which have the potential to improve student motivation and classroom learning. Four topics will be examined: Maslow's theory of motivation, the motivation to achieve, rewards and motivation, and implications for teachers.

Maslow's Hierachy of Needs

Motivation has been defined as the internal forces that initiate, direct, and sustain individual or group behavior in order to satisfy a need or attain a goal (16).

Maslow's (12) model of human motivation is the most frequently cited motivational theory in education literature. He suggested a hierachy of needs arranged in such a manner that each need becomes dominate when lower needs have been gratified. In order to study changes in student motivational structures during adolescence, Gnagey (9) operationalized Maslow's needs by relating them to specific activities as follows:

Needs	Activity
Physiological Needs	"Taking care of my own physical needs: food, clothing, shelter, etc."
Safety Needs	"Keeping safe and secure so that no one can hurt me."
Love and Belonging Needs	"Finding and keeping close friends who think a lot of me."
Esteem Needs	"Becoming a good person who is looked up to by others."
Self-Actualization Needs	"Pursuing hobbies that are satisfying to me."
Need to Know Needs	"Finding out about new things. Satisfying my curiosity."

Maslow contended that physiological needs, such as the need for food and water, will drive behavior more strongly than safety needs which are more powerful than love and belonging needs, and so forth. Maslow did not believe that each need must be absolutely and fully gratified in order for the next higher need to influence behavior. No behavior can be fully explained in terms of a single need nor can all behaviors and learning be analyzed in terms of motivation factors alone. Nevertheless, reference to Maslow's hierachy of needs provides classroom teachers some understanding of what motivates students.

Gnagey (9) conducted a study that focused exclusively on motivational changes that take place between the ages of 13 and 19. In general, his findings supported the hierarchical model proposed by Maslow and identified the predominate needs of seventh and eighth grade students. Boys at this age were found to be motivated most strongly by the need to know, followed by self actualization, physiological needs, love and belonging needs, esteem needs, and safety needs. Girls were most motivated by needs related to esteem followed by love and belonging, need to know, self actualization, physiological, and safety needs. Gnagey's interpretation of these findings suggested that middle school girls should be motivated by group work with their friends and respond well to activities and teacher comments that enhance their self-concepts. He claimed that it is probably important for middle school girls to have teachers that like them and communicate this affection clearly. Middle school boys, on the other hand, generally should be motivated by experiments, novel approaches, and puzzling situations which challenge their ability to understand and explain a particular event. According to Gnagey's findings, middle school teachers can expect most of their students will be motivated by learning activities aimed at satisfying higher level needs.

Establishing the Motivation to Achieve

Classroom teachers are concerned about their students' academic achievement and search for techniques that will enhance motivation to achieve. McCelland (14) studied achievement motivation with school age children and suggested three conditions which teachers should foster to improve academic motivation.

First, students must believe that they can learn or will develop the ability to achieve. No matter how much students want to be successful, they are likely to fail if they feel the instructional goals are beyond their capabilities.

Second, students are more likely to increase their academic motivation if they are given a clear idea of what must done in order to achieve the instructional goal. Directions must be concrete and specific in order to be of maximum benefit to the student.

Third, students must recognize how the goals of instruction relate to their everyday lives. Students need to experience a heightened sense of self-satisfaction when goals are achieved. The benefits of increased achievement must be clear to students in order to increase their motivation.

Teachers must be aware that achievement motivation is relevant only if students perceive themselves as responsible for their own learning and know that they will be evaluated against some standard of excellence. Furthermore, students face two conflicting motivations when deciding whether to attempt a prescribed learning task: one is the motivation to succeed and the other is the motivation to avoid failure. Teachers should realize that some students are "achievement oriented" while others are "failure oriented." Different approaches are likely to be effective with achievement oriented and failure oriented students. Achievement oriented students prefer tasks that are moderately difficult, neither too difficult nor too easy. Failure oriented students, on the other hand, may perceive easier tasks as sufficiently challenging and thus be more motivated to try them (6,13).

Alshuler (1) found that an optimum level of student motivation can be achieved by permitting students to establish their own goals and then grade them accordingly. He presented students with a learning task in the form of a self-competition game. Students set their own goals and were evaluated according to terms they set for themselves. This procedure was found to result in significant increases in the level of achievement on the task.

Extrinsic and Intrinsic Motivation

Frequently, teachers use extrinsic rewards as motivation for students to engage in academic tasks. Higher grades, awards, prizes, and membership in special organizations have been used to encourage academic involvement. Some reseachers frown on these practices and claim that the use of rewards reduces the desire to learn when the rewards are no longer available. (11)

Bates (2) conducted an extensive review of research related to extrinsic rewards and intrinsic motivation and concluded that rewards contingent only upon participating in an activity generally result in a decreased interest in that activity and doubted the wisdom of dispensing certificates or trophies for merely participating. In cases where task performance is already closely associated with extrinsic rewards, their removal would appear to be more damaging to intrinsic motivation than continuing them.

Bates (2) also found that social reinforcers, such as an encouraging word from the teacher or a pat on the back, may contribute to intrinsic motivation *if* they are salient to the task at hand and *if* their presentation is both unambiguous and occurs seldom enough to prevent satiation. These and other more natural reinforcers are probably of greatest value when the task to be rewarded is one not normally associated with a tangible reinforcer.

Current research suggests that in order to maintain student intrinsic motivation the use of extrinsic rewards must be carefully monitored. The granting of rewards should not occur when the learning task is of high interest to the student and would probably be completed without any external incentive. Rewards can be useful to motivate students when the learning task is of low interest and would not likely be completed without an external incentive (18).

Implications for Teachers

The implications of motivation research for classroom teachers have been very well summarized by Wlodkowski (19). He proposed a time continuum model for motivating students. The model suggests three stages during which the teacher can apply differential motivation techniques: 1) beginning of the lesson when the student enters and starts the learning process; 2) during the lesson when the student is involved in the body or main content of the learning process; and 3) ending of the lesson when the student is finishing or completing the learning process.

According to Wlodkowski, teachers should begin the learning process by developing more positive student attitudes toward the general learning environment, the teacher, the subject matter, and self, and by establishing that the content and skills to be learned will satisfy a basic need within the student. He suggests numerous techniques for accomplishing these ends.

During the learning process, the student must be stimulated to maintain attention to the instructional activity and the teacher must insure that the student is experiencing supportive affective or emotional results. This is particularly important with middle school age girls. At the end of the lesson, the student must be made aware of the increased competence that has resulted from the learning experience. Strategies for demonstrating self-competence are also presented by Wlodkowski who suggests several specific techniques to achieve these goals.

Research studies have shown relationships among classroom climate, student motivation and achievement. Moen and Doyle (15) demonstrated that supportive classroom climates increase student efforts, aspirations, and satisfaction with their educational experiences. Fry and Coe (7) found a significantly positive relationship between academic motivation and the classroom social climate for junior high school pupils. Chamberlin (4) claimed that the teacher's most significant contribution is to help students believe in their capabilities. She suggested the following rules of thumb to improve student motivation: avoid negativism, create success opportunities for students, relate to students as individuals, encourage risk taking, communicate concern for the student, and build student feelings of self-worth.

The research evidence suggests that teachers *can* influence student motivation and have a positive effect on learning in the classroom. Approaches for accomplishing this goal are well documented and effective instructional materials for improving teacher capabilities in this area are available (19). The task before us is to implement the strategies and techniques that will result in improved motivation and learning.

REFERENCES

1. Alshuler, A.S. *How to increase motivation through climate and structure* (Achievement Motivation Development Project Working Paper No. 8). Cambridge: Harvard University Graduate School of Education, 1968. Cited in Gibson, J.C. *Psychology for the classroom.* Englewood Cliffs, N.J.: Prentice Hall, Inc., 1976.
2. Bates, J.A. Extrinsic reward and intrinsic motivation: a review with implications for the classroom. *Review of Educational Research*, 1979, *49:4* 557-576.
3. Bruner, J.S. *Toward a Theory of Instruction.* New York: W. Norton, 1968.
4. Chamberlin, L.J. The greatest gift, *Childhood Education*, 1981, *58:1*, 2-7.
5. Cleland, D. Developing student interest through novelty and variety. *Journal of Physical Education and Recreation*, 1979, *50:5*, 39-40.
6. Feather, N.T. Persistence at a difficult task with alternative tasks of intermediate difficulty. *Journal of Abnormal and Social Psychology*, 1963, *66*, 604-609.
7. Fry, P.S. and Coe, K.J. Interactions among dimensions of academic motivation and classroom social climate: a study of the perceptions of junior high and high school pupils. *British Journal of Educational Psychology*, 1980, *50:1*, 33-42.
8. Gibson, Janice T. *Psychology for the classroom* Prentice Hall, Inc., Englewood Cliffs, N.J., 1976.
9. Gnagey, W.J. Changes in student motivational structure during adolescence. *Adolescence*, 1980, *WV:59*, 671-681.
10. Goodman, P. *Compulsory Mis-education.* New York: Random House, 1962.
11. Lepper, M.R., Green D., and Nisbeth, R.E. Understanding Children's intrinsic interest with extrinsic rewards. *Journal of Personality and Social Psychology*, 1973, *28*, 129-137.
12. McClelland, D.C. What is the effect of achievement motivation training in the schools? *Teachers College Record*, 1972, *74*, 129-145.
13. Maslow, A.H. *Toward a psychology of being.* Princeton, N.J.: Van Nostrand - Rinehold: 1968.
14. Moehr, M.L. and Sjogien, D.D. Atkinson's theory of achievement movitation: first step toward a theory of academic motivation. *Review of Educational Research*, 1971, *41*, 143-161.
15. Moen, R.E. and Doyle, K.O. Measures of academic motivation: a conceptional review. *Research in Higher Education*, 1978, *8*, 1-23.
16. *Thesaurus of ERIC Descriptors.* Phoenix, AR: Oryx Press: 1980.
17. Weiner, B. A theory of motivation for some classroom experiences. *Journal of Educational Psychology*, 1979, *71:1*, 3-25.
18. Wlodkowski, R.J. *What Research Says To The Teacher: Motivation.* Washington, D.C.: National Education Association, 1977.
19. Wlodkowski, R.J. *Motivation and Teaching: A Practical Guide.* Washington, D.C.: National Education Association, 1978.

2. Classroom Management

One of the middle school teacher's most important responsibilities is to manage the classroom so that opportunity for productive learning is increased. In fact, it may be argued that effective classroom management is a prerequisite for achieving any other instructional goal. A primary task for the classroom teacher, then, is to "gain and maintain cooperation in classroom activities" (Doyle, 1979). The repetoire of procedures by which the teacher gains and maintains this cooperation is called classroom management.

The most compelling reason for attending to classroom management is found in research suggesting that teachers who are effective classroom managers tend to produce more student learning (Brophy and Putnam, 1979). The logic of these findings is supported by a body of research which identifies the amount of time spent in direct academic instruction as one variable that is significantly and consistently related to academic achievement (Corno, 1979). Without doubt, effective classroom management procedures influence directly the amount of time spent in academic instruction and, therefore, affect student achievement as well.

Students expect teachers to manage classrooms efficiently for the purpose of maintaining productive learning environments. Markle (1977) and his colleagues found that middle school students rated as "important" those teacher behaviors associated with classroom management and discipline. Among the teacher behaviors associated with that factor were: "is strict," "is firm," and "is aware of what is happening in the classroom." Nash (1976) concluded that children in British schools expected teachers to "keep order," "teach you," "explain," and be "fair, interesting, and friendly." In a survey of literature on teacher characteristics associated with effective classroom management, Brophy and Putnam (1979) concluded that it is helpful if teachers are liked by their students. Characteristic of the ego strength which students admired in teachers was an underlying self-confidence that enables teachers to "(a) remain calm in crisis, (b) listen actively without becoming defensive or authoritarian, (c) avoid win-lose conflicts, and (d) maintain a problem-solving orientation rather than resort to blaming, hysteria or other emotional characteristics."

Much of the research on classroom management may be conveniently divided into three topical areas: management problems which arise from instructional difficulties, those which develop from a lack of group cohesiveness, and those which stem from the problems of individual students. Notably, the research in all categories supports the position that the real difference between successful and unsuccessful classroom managers lies not in their responses to misbehavior, but in the planning that goes into effective instruction. Additional differences are found in the techniques of group management used by teachers to maintain attention and prevent disruption rather than in the terminating behaviors that are offered in response to student disruptive behavior (Kounin, 1970).

Frequently, student misbehavior occurs as a result of inattention to management issues in the planning of instruction. Kounin reported that classroom management problems will be caused by any factor which results in delay or confusion. More specifically, student inattention and misbehavior were most often traced to a lack of continuity in the lesson, a problem that emerged from inadequate teacher preparation. This difficulty was especially noticeable during the "transition" phases of lessons, the times at which the class was changing topics or activities. Conversely, students remained attentive when the instructional activities were ordered logically and moved at a reasonable pace. Management problems, Kounin found, increased when teachers wandered from the topic for no apparent reason, repeated and reviewed material that the students already understood, paused to gather their thoughts or prepare materials, or deal with other concerns that could have been postponed. As might be expected, independent work or "seatwork" proved to be of little value in preventing misbehavior if it offered no challenge or was repetitive or lacking in variation.

Clearly, research on the instructional correlates of classroom management calls for students to be *actively* engaged in processing new information or some other activity which presents a challenge, some variety, and a promise of successful completion. Careful instructional planning, with special attention given to the manner in which transitions are to be made, will reduce the likelihood that students will be presented with the opportunity to behave in a disruptive fashion.

As in any other social situation, the classroom group depends on a certain amount of cohesiveness to maintain order. Order, as it relates to classroom management, may be defined as a "situation where there is a clear set of expectations for all classroom members, where people can anticipate how others will behave, where people feel that it is right and proper for everyone to conform to these expectations, and where there is a high degree of conformity to the expectations" (Cohen et al., 1979). Order in the classroom, therefore, requires not only clearly defined procedures or expectations, but a commitment on the part of group members to common goals and standards. Effective groups show cohesiveness and positive attitudes among members toward one another (Stafford, 1971). Specific management activities can and must be employed in order to build the group cohesiveness upon which individual commitment and order depend.

Brophy and Putnam (1979) report that there is disagreement over how involved students should be in the formation of classroom rules. Glasser (1969) suggests that students of middle school age are prepared for participation in the formation of classroom rules, but that the teacher must act as guide so that unreasonable rules are not created. Most of the research, however, suggests that *as a minimum* students must understand the rationale for specific rules and accept their reasonableness as well as understanding the rule itself. Upon summarizing research on classroom rules, Brophy and Putnam offer three caveats: rules should be kept to a minimum number, they should be flexible, and they should be stated as general qualitative behavioral guides rather than specific do's and don't's. Glasser (1969) adds that a mechanism for changing outdated, unreasonable or unworkable rules should also exist in the middle school classroom.

In a now classic study with middle school aged boys, Lewin (1939) and his colleagues investigated the effects of leaders' style on task achievement and group cohesiveness. He found that authoritarian leaders were effective in achieving tasks, but at the price of much tension and the general antipathy of group members toward one another and the leader. Democratic leaders, those who solicited opinions and worked toward consensus, caused only slightly lower group productivity but generated warm feelings among group members and toward the leader. When leaders acted in a laissez-faire manner, giving vague directions and sketchy answers, both task performance and affective qualities suffered. Recognizing the practical limitations of the democratic leadership style for all school activities, Baumrind (1971) advanced a modified version of the democratic style, called the authoritative leader, as being appropriate for school settings. She concluded that the effective classroom leader is in a position of authority and responsibility, speaks as a mature and experienced adult, and retains ultimate decision power. However, this type of leader also solicits opinions, seeks consensus, and makes sure that everyone understands the reasons for the group's decisions and activity.

Johnson (1970) reports that teachers can promote classroom group cohesiveness by arranging for cooperative experiences, minimizing competition among class members, promoting pro-social behavior and helping each member of the class identify with the class as a whole. Kounin (1970) offers specific empirically supported recommendations for teachers who wish to improve their group management techniques. Teachers should demonstrate "withitness," a continuous awareness of what is happening throughout the classroom; "overlapping," or the ability to do more than one thing at a time; smoothness of transition from one activity to another; and "group alerting" behavior, essentially verbal cues that keep the entire group attentive while one class member is reciting or responding to a question.

A final caution regarding the teacher's attempts to build group cohesiveness is offered by Brophy and Putnam. In essence, the teacher is attempting to exercise leadership over an intact group of students which has established peer leadership. It is imperative that the teacher gain the confidence and cooperation of the existing group leadership in order to avoid conflicting with them or causing them to lose face.

Despite the best attempts of teachers to plan appropriate instruction and build a sense of group cohesiveness, occasional incidents of individual disruptive behavior are inevitable. Two general sets of teacher response to this behavior are possible: behavior modification or the application of consultative techniques.

Behavior modification operates on the principles of reward and reinforcement associated with operant conditioning. Desirable behavior is consistently rewarded so that it will be repeated; undesirable behavior is not rewarded in order to effect its eventual extinction. The debate over behavior modification continues to rage, with advocates citing its effectiveness in coping with extreme maladaptive behavior and detractors offering equally compelling arguments in opposition to its mechanistic and manipulative qualities. On one point, though, most researchers agree: punishment is notably ineffective as a basic approach to socialization (Brophy, 1977). The use of punishment may be useful for inhibiting undesirable behavior for short periods of time, but is generally ineffective as a means for encouraging students to accept responsibility for and monitor their own behavior (O'Leary and O'Leary, 1977).

Of special interest to classroom teachers are the conditions under which behavior modificaton approaches must operate in order to be effective. Behavior modification is, by definition, a technique which is designed for individuals rather than groups (Emery and Marholin, 1977). Therefore, precise behavioral monitoring, systematic reward and gradual withdrawal of the reward system become genuine practical problems for the teacher who works with large groups of students. In addition, there is considerable difficulty in identifying rewards which are truly rewarding for the children receiving them (Brophy and Putnam, 1979). Not all

3. Classroom Groups

Teachers manage and work with more groups than any other profession. Classes exist as groups, instruction is delivered to groups, and the organization of schools is based upon groups of varying sizes and functions. Among middle school students, attention to group behavior is especially important since the peer group begins to emerge as a major influence on individual school behavior, offering for the first time a significant alternative to parental and other adult influences.

Unfortunately, less attention is given to the formation and management of classroom groups than to the preparation of content and instructional methods. However, the theoretical and empirical connections between group dynamics and student performance are clear. Successful groups contribute to student achievement, effective classroom management, and generally positive attitudes toward school; unsuccessful or ineffective groups increase hostility and tension, precipitate behavior problems, and contribute to negative attitudes toward school and learning.

All groups have a leader. If the "legislated leader" — the teacher — fails to provide leadership because of inattention to group processes another leader will emerge. If this leader's purposes are in conflict with the purposes of schooling, classroom ambiance and academic learning suffer immeasurable harm.

Several dimensions of group behavior are especially worthy of attention by the classroom teacher: group norms and rules, group expectations, and group cohesiveness. Each of these dimensions may be influenced by the teacher, and each has been linked, theoretically and empirically, to school behavior and performance. It is important for teachers to understand both the unique dimensions of each of these concepts *and* the manner in which they relate to one another to influence the chemistry of a particular group of students.

Group norms are "shared expectations or attitudes about what are appropriate procedures and behaviors" (Schmuck and Schmuck, 1975). These "norms are established by the group to maintain behavioral consistency" (Shaw, 1971). In most groups, norms do not describe *specific* behavioral expectations but general qualitative guides for behavior. Shaw (1971) says, for example, it is unlikely that any group would adhere to a norm which specified that all members must say "good morning" upon greeting another group member. It is more likely that the norm would require a cordial greeting, but would not mandate a specific behavior.

Group norms which are characterized by narrow limits of tolerable behavior mean that the liklihood of running afoul of a group norm is increased. Among groups where the ranges of tolerable behavior are broad, there is a tone of encouragement and mutual support; in groups where tolerance is limited to a few behavioral options, restraint, rigidity and anxiety are prevalent (Jackson, 1960). In short, groups which provide very specific behavorial options for their members tend to increase anxiety in individual members. Classroom rules which are perceived as narrow, petty and very specific are unlikely to become group norms for the students, especially if they are not agreed upon by members of the class. Rules which are formed about things that are significant to the group, that are accepted by group members, and that exhibit fairly broad ranges of tolerable behavior are most likely to become group norms (Shaw, 1977; Schmuck and Schmuck, 1975). Once formed, these norms influence involvement in academic work and the nature practical limitations of the democratic leadership style for all school activities, Baumrind (1971) advanced a modified version of the democratic style, called the authoritative leader, as being appropriate for school settings. She concluded that the effective classroom leader is in a position of authority and responsibility, speaks as a mature and experienced adult, and retains ultimate decision power. However, this type of leader also solicits opinions, seeks consensus, and makes sure that everyone understands the reasons for the group's decisions and activity.

Johnson (1970) reports that teachers can promote classroom group cohesiveness by arranging for cooperative experiences, minimizing competition among class members, promoting pro-social behavior and helping each member of the class identify with the class as a whole. Kounin (1970) offers specific empirically supported recommendations for teachers who wish to improve their group management techniques. Teachers should demonstrate "withitness," a continuous awareness of what is happening throughout the classroom; "overlapping," or the ability to do more than one thing at a time; smoothness of transition from one activity to another; and "group alerting" behavior, essentially verbal cues that keep the entire group attentive while one class member is reciting or responding to a question.

A final caution regarding the teacher's attempts to build group cohesiveness is offered by Brophy and Putnam. In essence, the teacher is attempting to exercise leadership over an intact group of students which has established peer leadership. It is imperative that the teacher gain the confidence and cooperation of the existing group leadership in order to avoid conflicting with them or causing them to lose face.

Despite the best attempts of teachers to plan appropriate instruction and build a sense of group cohesiveness, occasional incidents of individual disruptive behavior are inevitable. Two general sets of teacher response to this behavior are possible: behavior modification or the application of consultative techniques.

Behavior modification operates on the principles of reward and reinforcement associated with operant conditioning. Desirable behavior is consistently rewarded so that it will be repeated; undesirable behavior is not rewarded in order to effect its eventual extinction. The debate over behavior modification continues to rage, with advocates citing its effectiveness in coping with extreme maladaptive behavior and detractors offering equally compelling arguments in opposition to its mechanistic and manipulative qualities. On one point, though, most researchers agree: punishment is notably ineffective as a basic approach to socialization (Brophy, 1977). The use of punishment may be useful for inhibiting undesirable behavior for short periods of time, but is generally ineffective as a means for encouraging students to accept responsibility for and monitor their own behavior (O'Leary and O'Leary, 1977).

Of special interest to classroom teachers are the conditions under which behavior modificaton approaches must operate in order to be effective. Behavior modification is, by definition, a technique which is designed for individuals rather than groups (Emery and Marholin, 1977). Therefore, precise behavioral monitoring, systematic reward and gradual withdrawal of the reward system become genuine practical problems for the teacher who works with large groups of students. In addition, there is considerable difficulty in identifying rewards which are truly rewarding for the children receiving them (Brophy and Putnam, 1979). Not all students respond similarly to teacher praise or to specified tokens. In a middle school setting, this problem is compounded by the shift of student interest away from adults and toward the peer group as a valued source of reward and reinforcement (Kieffer and Johnston, 1979).

The effect of the extrinsic reinforcement system which is essential to the behavior modification technique has been examined by Edward Deci (1975). He reports that the use of an extrinsic reward for specific behavior reduces the intrinsic motivation to perform the same behavior. Sustained performance of the behavior, then, becomes dependent upon external reinforcement in the future. Results of research on the long term effect of behavior modification on behavior change or the transfer of learning to other situations is, presently, inconclusive and not very promising (Brophy and Putnam, 1979).

More promising for the classroom teacher is the research which investigates the use of various consultative techniques in responding to disruptive behavior. There is much evidence that negative teacher behaviors such as unrelenting criticism, sarcasm, blame, withdrawal of privileges, isolation and corporal punishment actually increase and reinforce disruptive behavior (Thompson et al., 1974; Flanders, 1970; Ginott, 1972). Conversely, teacher behaviors such as active listening, judicious praise, empathic response, and sincere counseling reduce instances of undesirable behavior.

After reviewing research on teachers as listeners, Dunkin and Biddle (1974) concluded that as many as one-third of students' answers to questions are inappropriate to the question that was asked. One-fifth of the answers that teachers accepted were not consistent with the questions they had asked. In the face of that data, the research on active listening becomes even more important. Teachers who listen, and who indicate to the student that they *heard* what he said by paraphrasing the student's comment or asking a question directly related to the student's statement, have significantly fewer management problems. More specifically, these confirming responses tend to prevent escalation of hostility, aggression and defensiveness. Generally, a teacher response which indicates active listening and empathy results in the greater likelihood of agreement between the teacher and student. Even when agreement was not reached, student perceptions of being understood reduced hostility (Johnson, n.d.; Ginott, 1972; Gordon, 1975).

In many teaching situations, there is a shortage of genuine and sincere praise; most teacher comments may be considered affectively neutral (Dunkin and Biddle, 1974; Flanders, 1970). Praise and approval can be useful in managing young adolescent classrooms provided that the praise is neither effusive nor perfunctory. Praise is most effective when it is related to a specific, identified behavior ("I appreciate your help with the bulletin board" rather than "You're a good boy."), and when it is task oriented ("You're doing a good job on those problems.") (House, 1970; Gnagey, n.d.; Goldenson, 1970). Given the peer pressure on young adolescents, it is sometimes wise to give praise privately.

Among the most promising approaches to classroom management is a school-adapted version of reality therapy developed by William Glasser. In this system, students help set rules, adjust them when necessary and deal with discipline problems. The role of the teacher is one of helping the student assess his own behavior, determine its appropriateness, and plan corrective strategies. Results of Glasser's

(1977) research indicates that this system has resulted in reductions in office referrals, fighting and suspensions.

It is clear that no cookbook exists for classroom management. Several principles emerge from the research, however, which are of direct utility to teachers. Most management problems can be prevented through careful planning of instructional activity and specific attention to building group cohesiveness. Problems of individual misbehavior are handled most effectively with careful listening, empathy, and a specific plan for correction. The complexity of human relations and interactions associated with classroom management mitigate against a "formula" approach to management problems. It is more appropriate for teachers to internalize general principles of human development and behavior and to be guided by those principles in their interactions with students.

REFERENCES

Baumrind, Diana. Current patterns of parental authority. *Developmental Psychology Monograph in Developmental Psychology,* IV: Part 2, 1-103, 1971.

Brophy, Jere E. *Child development and socialization,* Chicago: Science Research Associates, 1977.

Brophy, Jere E. and Joyce G. Putnam. Classroom management in the elementary grades, in *Classroom Management,* The Seventy-Eighth Yearbook of the National Society for the Study of Education, ed. Daniel L. Duke, Chicago: University of Chicago Press, 1979.

Cohen, Elizabeth G., Jo-Ann K. Intili and Susan Hurevitz Robbins. Task and authority: a sociological view of classroom management, in *Classroom management,* the Seventy-Eighth Yearbook of the National Society for the Study of Education, ed. Daniel L. Duke, Chicago: University of Chicago Press, 1979,

Corno, Lyn. Classroom instruction and the matter of time, in *Classroom management,* The Seventy-Eighth Yearbook of the National Society for the Study of Education, ed. Daniel L. Duke, Chicago: University of Chicago Press, 1979.

Deci, Edward L. *Intrinsic motivation,* New York: Plenum Press, 1975.

Doyle, Walter. Making managerial decisions in classrooms, in *Classroom management,* The Seventy-Eighth Yearbook of the National Society for the Study of Education, ed. Daniel L. Duke, Chicago: University of Chicago Press, 1979.

Dunkin, Michael J. and Bruce J. Biddle. *The study of teaching.* New York: Holt, Rinehart and Winston, 1974.

Emery, Robert E. and David Marholin. An applied behavior analysis of deliquency, *American Psychologist,* 32, 860-73, 1977

Flanders, Ned A. *Analyzing teacher behavior,* Reading, MA: Addison-Wesley Publishing Co., 1970.

Ginott, Haim. *Teacher and child,* New York: Avon Books, 1972.

Glasser, William. *Schools without failure,* New York: Harper and Row, 1969.

Glasser, William. Ten steps to good discipline, *Todays Education,* 66 (November-December, 1977) 61-63, 1977.

Gnagey, William J. Controlling classroom misbehavior, *What research says to the teacher series,* No. 32, ERIC ED 077 899.

Goldenson, Robert M. *The encyclopedia of human behavior: psychology, psychiatry and mental health,* Garden City: Doubleday & Company, 1970.

Gordon, Thomas, *Teacher effectiveness training,* New York: Wyden Press, 1975.

Howe, Michael. A humanizing approach to teacher control in the classroom, *National Elementary Principal 49, 1970.*

Johnson, David W. The efficacy of role reversal, warmth of interaction, accuracy of understanding, and the proposal of compromises, University of Minnesota, ERIC ED 044 729.

Johnson, David W. *The social psychology of education,* New York: Holt, Rinehart and Winston, 1970.

Kieffer, Leigh F. and J. Howard Johnston, For middle school education: back to the most basic of basics, *N.A.S.S.P. Bulletin,* 63 (May, 1979): 73-80.

Kounin, Jacob S. *Discipline and group management in classrooms,* New York: Holt, Rinehart and Winston, 1970.

Lewin, Kurt, Ronald Lippitt and Robert K. White, Patterns of aggressive behavior in experimentally created social climates, *Journal of Social Psychology,* 10: 271-299, (1939).

Markle, Glenn C., J. Howard Johnston, James Hogan and Donald Smith. Students' perception of the ideal middle school teacher, *Middle School Journal,* 8: 6-7, 1977.

Nash, Roy. Pupil expectations of their teachers, in *Explorations in Classroom Observation,* ed. Michael Stubbs and Sara Delamont, New York: John Wiley and Sons, 1976.

O'Leary, Daniel K. and Susan G. O'Leary. *Classroom management: the successful use of behavior modification,* 2nd ed., New York: Pergamon Press, 1977.

Rogers, Carl. *Client centered therapy.* Boston: Houghton-Mifflin, 1951.

Stafford, Gene. *Developing effective classroom groups: a practical guide for teachers,* New York: Hart Publishing Co., 1971.

Thompson, Marion, et al., Contingency management in the schools: how often and how well does it work? *American Educational Research Journal,* 11, 1974.

August, 1979

3. Classroom Groups

Teachers manage and work with more groups than any other profession. Classes exist as groups, instruction is delivered to groups, and the organization of schools is based upon groups of varying sizes and functions. Among middle school students, attention to group behavior is especially important since the peer group begins to emerge as a major influence on individual school behavior, offering for the first time a significant alternative to parental and other adult influences.

Unfortunately, less attention is given to the formation and management of classroom groups than to the preparation of content and instructional methods. However, the theoretical and empirical connections between group dynamics and student performance are clear. Successful groups contribute to student achievement, effective classroom management, and generally positive attitudes toward school; unsuccessful or ineffective groups increase hostility and tension, precipitate behavior problems, and contribute to negative attitudes toward school and learning.

All groups have a leader. If the "legislated leader" — the teacher — fails to provide leadership because of inattention to group processes another leader will emerge. If this leader's purposes are in conflict with the purposes of schooling, classroom ambiance and academic learning suffer immeasurable harm.

Several dimensions of group behavior are especially worthy of attention by the classroom teacher: group norms and rules, group expectations, and group cohesiveness. Each of these dimensions may be influenced by the teacher, and each has been linked, theoretically and empirically, to school behavior and performance. It is important for teachers to understand both the unique dimensions of each of these concepts *and* the manner in which they relate to one another to influence the chemistry of a particular group of students.

Group norms are "shared expectations or attitudes about what are appropriate procedures and behaviors" (Schmuck and Schmuck, 1975). These "norms are established by the group to maintain behavioral consistency" (Shaw, 1971). In most groups, norms do not describe *specific* behavioral expectations but general qualitative guides for behavior. Shaw (1971) says, for example, it is unlikely that any group would adhere to a norm which specified that all members must say "good morning" upon greeting another group member. It is more likely that the norm would require a cordial greeting, but would not mandate a specific behavior.

Group norms which are characterized by narrow limits of tolerable behavior mean that the liklihood of running afoul of a group norm is increased. Among groups where the ranges of tolerable behavior are broad, there is a tone of encouragement and mutual support; in groups where tolerance is limited to a few behavioral options, restraint, rigidity and anxiety are prevalent (Jackson, 1960). In short, groups which provide very specific behavorial options for their members tend to increase anxiety in individual members. Classroom rules which are perceived as narrow, petty and very specific are unlikely to become group norms for the students, especially if they are not agreed upon by members of the class. Rules which are formed about things that are significant to the group, that are accepted by group members, and that exhibit fairly broad ranges of tolerable behavior are most likely to become group norms (Shaw, 1977; Schmuck and Schmuck, 1975). Once formed, these norms influence involvement in academic work and the nature of the interactions among group members. They also permit members to monitor and adjust their own behavior as well as that of other individuals in the group.

Group norms exert a powerful influence on a number of phenomena related to classroom instruction. Student perception, or the way in which student views his or her world, is among the most dramatically affected. If a student group decides that mathematics is "hard" or boring" or "confusing", they will, doubtless, focus their attention on the hardest, most boring and confusing of its elements. Cognitive norms, the way a group thinks about something, may lead students to look for right/wrong, true/false answers to ambiguous questions, thereby frustrating the teacher who hopes to develop student abilities to contend with ambiguity. Evaluative norms prescribe favorable or unfavorable group responses to events or behaviors. The cruel treatment of a handicapped student might be punished severely by one group and rewarded by another. A specific rock group might be "in" with one group and "out" with another, as might science or yo-yos or sports. Behavioral norms, those that guide an individual's overt actions, are generally comprised of perceptual, cognitive and evaluative norms (Schmuck and Schmuck, 1975). Asch's (1952) classical experiments involving the willingness of subjects to deny their own sensory perceptions in favor of an obviously incorrect answer offered by another group members shows just how dramatically a group may influence student behavior. Interestingly, though, the influence might be quite superficial. If a youngster is not in the presence of peers, he is not nearly as likely to demonstrate behavior that has not been internalized, even though he demonstrates it in a group setting.

Norms may be influenced by a teacher. Perceptual norms, although among the most tenacious, can be altered through persistent presentation of "evidence" that contradicts the norm. If a student group perceives teachers as sarcastic and cruel, the way to change that perceptual norm is to be sincere and kind. Unproductive cognitive norms, especially those dealing with the learning process, can be altered by including students in the intellectual life of the classroom, the planning of objectives, the selection of content and the evaluation of learning activities. Teaching the methods of inquiry germane to a given subject also help produce positive cognitive norms. Evaluative norms should be examined by the group as a whole. Teachers should be especially sensitive to norms which isolate and restrict certain group members and make an active attempt to have the group confront those norms. Behavorial norms are among the easiest to modify. They can be altered by engaging students in discussion about how group pressure may have prohibited or enhanced effectiveness, efficiency and productivity (Schmuck and Schmuck, 1975).

Congruence between group norms and individual behavior is extremely important, especially among young adolescents. Hoffman (1957) found, for example, that people experience anxiety when their personal responses are at variance with group norms; the greater the variance, the greater the anxiety. For this reason, teachers must be aware that it may not be productive to require students to behave in ways that are at variance with group norms unless some attention has been given to adjustment of those norms.

Closely related to the concept norm is that of *group expectation*. Expectations are predictions of how another person (or group) will behave. Lippit (1962) has argued that expectations are based upon assessments. Teachers may "assess" a group of students and find them to have low IQ scores, set expectations of limited performance in accordance with those IQ scores, treat students as if they are incapable of independent thought, find that they are and reconfirm their initial assessments about "low-IQ" kids. Evidence of this assessment-expectation-treatment-confirmation syndrome is abundant (Palardy, 1969; Brophy and Good, 1970).

It should not be inferred, though, that expectations usually have negative effects on learning. White (1959) described expectations as "a necessary component of every individual's motive for competency." According to White, people define personal achievement in terms of some situation, person or group. In order to act competently, people must have an objective view of their immediate environment. They must know, in other words, what is expected of them.

Unfortunately, the assessments upon which expectations are based are not always entirely accurate. Faculty lounge comments about students and lunchroom assessments of teachers often predispose teachers and students to act toward one another in prejudicial ways. If a teacher expects a student to be uncooperative and surly, the student is almost certain to be so. If a group of students expects a teacher to be mean and cynical, they will be certain to precipitate those behaviors and perceive them as the dominant structure of that teacher's personality.

For the most part, accurate expectations of others are gained by repeated interactions with them. Other, generally less accurate, ways of establishing expectations are by gathering information about people (through the grapevine), responding to cultural stereotypes ("blacks are..."), and basing expectations on situational variables ("If you're in the discipline office, you must be a discipline problem") (Schmuck and Schmuck, 1975).

Because expectations are so important, it is essential that a teacher assess the expectations that students hold for her and her subject. If the expectations are counterproductive to learning, the teacher must use attitude adjustment techniques to modify those expectations. At the same time, it is essential that she establish expectations that are reasonable, forthright and congruent with existing or adjusted group norms.

Group cohesiveness is a concept that is concerned with feelings group members have about the group and the extent to which they want to remain members of the group. To a large degree, group cohesiveness results from acceptance of and adherence to group norms (Schmuck, 1966).

Groups which exhibit high cohesiveness tend to engage in more objective problem-solving behavior (French, 1941), devoting time to developing a task completion plan that all group members are likely to follow. Low cohesive groups, on the other hand, are more likely to avoid planning and begin to "test" one another almost at once (Shaw, 1975). Whereas members of high cohesive groups tend to be cooperative and friendly, often praising one another for achievements, low cohesive groups are often hostile and aggressive with members delighting in the errors of others (Shaw, 1962). Members of cohesive groups conform more to group norms than members of non-cohesive groups (Festinger et al., 1950), and a cohesive group is much more efficient in achieving its goals (Shaw, 1971).

For the school, group cohesiveness presents a double-edged sword. While highly cohesive groups tend to be more productive, more satisfied with group membership and more positive toward the institution that houses the group, they are also highly successful in resisting goals and procedures that violate group norms (Shaw, 1971). Therefore, it is important that institutions not attempt to impose arbitrary norms on highly cohesive groups.

Teachers can contribute to group cohesiveness by arranging for cooperative experiences, minimizing competition among group members, promoting pro-social behavior and helping each member to identify with the group as a whole (Johnson, 1972). Fowler (1979) and his colleagues suggest that teachers should conduct discussions to identify clear, mutually understood goals; make deliberate efforts to accept and support each student and encourage empathy among students; share the leadership function with the group; and focus attention on the group by directing students to talk to the group and not just the teacher, directing members to listen to one another, and using references such as "we", "us" and "our" when describing the group. Fowler concludes that teachers reduce group cohesiveness by reprimanding the wrong student, stopping a less serious deviancy when a more serious one is taking place, hesitating to stop misbehavior, and giving excessive public, verbal rewards to any one student.

Groups are among the most powerful forces influencing our intellectual, emotional and social lives. In fact, we live our lives in relatively small groups that have a demonstrated impact on our perceptions, attitudes and behavior. The group can solidify positions we already hold or change our positions completely (Myers, 1979). Such an influential force, given proper attention, can become a powerful ally in the learning process. Inattention to the dynamics of the groups we create in schools can lead to student failure, teacher frustration and instructional ineffectiveness.

REFERENCES

Asch, S.E. *Social Psychology*, Englewood Cliffs: Prentice-Hall, 1952.

Bach, K.W. Influence through social communication, *Journal of Abnormal and Social Psychology*, 46:9-23, 1951.

Brophy, Jere and T. Good. Teachers' communication of different expectations for children's classroom performance: some behavioral data, *Journal of Educational Psychology*, 61:365-74, 1970.

Festinger, L., S. Schehter and K.W. Back. *Social Pressure in Informal Groups*, New York: Harper, 1950.

Fowler, T.W., R.E. Sterling, G.C. Markle and J.H. Johnston, Rules for establishing and maintaining group cohesiveness, unpublished paper, University of Cincinnati, 1979.

French, J.R.P. The disruption and cohesion of groups, *Journal of Abnormal and Social Psychology*, 36:361-377, 1941.

Hoffman, M.L. Conformity as a defense mechanism and a form of resistance to genuine group influence, *Journal of Personality*, 25:412-424, 1957.

Jackson, J.M. Structural characteristics of norms, in Henry, Nelson B. (ed.) *The Dynamics of Instructional Groups*, 59th Yearbook, part 2, Chicago: National Society for the Study of Education, 1960.

Johnson, D.W. *Reaching Out: Interpersonal Effectiveness and Self-Actualization*, Englewood Cliffs: Prentice-Hall, 1972.

Lippitt, R. Unplanned maintenance and planned change in the group work process, in *Social Work Practice*, New York: Columbia University Press, 1962.

Myers, David G. How groups intensify opinions, *Human Nature*, March 1979.

Palardy, J.M. What teachers believe, what children achieve, *Elementary School Journal*, April, 1969.

Schmuck, R.A. Some aspects of classroom social climate, *Psychology in the Schools*, 3:59-65, 1966.

Schmuck, Richard A. and Patricia Schmuck, *Group Processes in the Classroom*, second ed., Dubuque, Iowa: W.C. Brown, Co., 1975.

Shaw, Marvin E. *Group Dynamics*, New York: McGraw-Hill, 1971

Shaw, M.E. and L.M. Shaw. Some effects of sociometric grouping upon learning in a second grade classroom, *Journal of Social Psychology*, 57:453-458, 1962.

White, R.W. Motivation reconsidered: the concept of competence, *Psychological Review*, 66:297-333, 1959.

February, 1980

4. Peer Relationships in the Classroom*

Writers and teachers note frequently the importance of the peer group to early adolescent students. The nature of the relationship of social status and peer relationships to performance, behavior, and attitudes in the classroom is less commonly agreed upon. The following information is taken from research efforts which included students at some level of the 10-to-14-age range within study groups, and which may therefore be of particular interest to middle school educators.

Research suggests that a first step in becoming rejected by peers at school is often a matter of nonachievement (3). If it is true that the student who achieves is more likely to be accepted, it is not so important for the teacher to work on acceptability, as such, but on achievement, the lack of which seems to precipitate rejection in many instances. Achievement has also been investigated in relation to the student's awareness of his position in the status system of the class.

Students who were accurate in estimating their position in a liking structure and who were negatively placed within that structure were lower utilizers of academic abilities and had less positive attitudes toward themselves and toward schools than did pupils who accurately estimated their position in the liking structure and who were positively placed in that structure. Those students who perceived themselves as being liked, although they actually had low liking status, used their abilities more effectively and had more positive attitudes toward self and school than those students who had low status and knew it (19).

Once obtained, a high social status within the classroom peer group may affect the student's achievement status. Mozdoerz, McDonville, and Krauss found that the academic performance of students with high social status within the classroom peer group tended to be consistently overestimated by peers, while the reverse pattern was observed for students with low social status (10).

The process of obtaining popularity within the classroom peer group may require certain behaviors on the part of the student. Hollander and Marcia found that popularity among fifth-grade males was enhanced by behavior showing independence from adult authority (e.g., not doing what teacher thinks is right). Popularity for females appears related to cooperation with adult authority figures. The study suggested that females, unlike males, can gain the approval of both peers and adults by conforming to a single standard of behavior (6).

Popularity with peers may also be related to physical appearance. The student who is heavy may be at a significant disadvantage. A study by Richardson found early adolescent males and females between the ages of 10 and 13 to be more prejudiced against fatness than against either facial disfigurement or body deformity (15).

Teachers may find that early adolsecent students of all status levels prefer peers to adults as sources of validation. Torrance presented subjects with various academic problems of a challenging nature, and found that fifth-graders preferred to check the accuracy of their answers with peers rather than adults. Torrance suggested that the need for consensual validation of peers lasts throughout preadolescence and may tend to reduce originality of expression and generally

*Dr. Lucille Freeman assisted in the preparation of this column.

decrease the output of ideas and questions from students who hesitate to think until they have checked with peers (22).

Entering a classroom peer group as a new student may be more difficult for females than males. Female subjects in a study by Sones and Feshback displayed more negative, rejecting attitudes toward same-sex strangers than did males. Specifically, females took longer to verbally acknowledge the newcomer's presence than did males, and were more inclined than males to ignore the newcomer's suggestions (21)

Within the class group, low sociometric status appears to be associated with low rates of verbal participation (1). Whether high sociometric status causes a student to be more vocal, or whether the high rate of verbal participation on the part of the student causes the student to achieve a high sociometric status is unclear.

Sociometric status also appears related to task orientation in a curvilinear manner. Schiffler used a sociometric measure to identify students with low, moderate, and high status. The moderate sociometric status group was the highest of the three groups in task orientation (18).

The effects of class size, classroom organization (open or structured), and grade level upon the friendship patterns of students were examined in a study by Hallinan, who collected cross-sectional sociometric data from 51 sixth, seventh, and eighth grades, and longitudinal data from 11 fourth, fifth, and sixth grades. Grade level appeared to have a strong effect on stability of friendships with all but one of the stable cliques identified occuring at the fifth or sixth-grade levels; open classes contained more social isolates than structured classes, perhaps because the freer interaction in open classrooms made students more knowledgeable of social sanctions for inappropriate friendship choices; and the average number of students who received no friendship choices was least at the sixth-grade level and greatest at the eighth-grade level (5).

Interestingly, more accurate information about the acceptability of students by their peers can be obtained from the students themselves than from the judgments of teachers. Moreno found a constantly decreasing figure for teachers, from that of being 62.5 percent accurate at the kindergarten level to that of being only 25 percent accurate at the seventh-grade level. At the eighth-grade level, teacher accuracy increased to 40 percent (9).

When teachers and peers are asked to rate the classroom behavior of a student, the ratings of teachers and peers tend to be quite similar and differ considerably from the student's preception and rating of his own behavior. Both teachers and peers tended to judge the results or consequences of behavior, whereas the student tended to judge the feelings and attitudes underlying his behavior (23). This different perspective may make it difficult for the student to judge which behaviors are likely to be approved or disapproved by others in the class.

Approval of significant others in the classroom situation has been shown to be related to an increase in self-ratings and in increase in preference for activities connected with a task, while disapproval of significant others appears to result in lower self-ratings and a decreased preference for related activities (8). The student's experience in the class may be positively affected not only by the degree to which he receives approval from peers, but also by opportunities to act as a leader of peers. Being placed in a leadership position within the classroom appears to reduce the tendency of fourth, fifth and sixth-grade students' negative attitudes and behaviors to become increasingly negative (25).

Several studies investigated the relationship between social status of the student and quality of interaction with the teacher. Lippitt and Gold observed that teachers of students at the kindergarten through the sixth-grade levels tended to pay attention to the social behavior, rather than the performance behavior, of students with low social status more often than they did of students with high social status. Low status males tended to receive more criticism than their high status male classmates, while low status females tended to receive more "support" from the teacher (7).

The degree to which teachers are aware of and can alter differential patterns of interaction with students such as those just cited was investigated by Withall. Twenty-six students in an eighth-grade art class at the University of Chicago Laboratory School and their teacher served as subjects for the study. Most classes were 75 minutes in length and three were 35 minutes in length. Great differences in teacher-student patterns of interaction were recorded. One student in the class received the teacher's attention once a minute, while another received the teacher's attention only once every half hour. Several students who received fewer teacher contacts were low status students in relation to the social system. For example, Subject "Q" was "...a fringer in the peer group, was rejected by boys, had more than her share of pubescent problems, was the youngest in the class, had the highest I.Q., was ungainly, overweight, and not a member of a well-knit clique..." When the teacher tried to decrease the imbalance in the teacher-student contacts within the classroom, he was only partially successful (24).

Polansky also examined teacher-student interactions to determine whether or not classrooms identified as having good climates were characterized by teachers who supported the existing group social status system. Withall's Climate Index was used to identify the degree to which the teacher was verbally supportive of each student. This information, viewed in relation to the sociometric status of students, enabled the researcher to determine the degree to which the teacher could be said to be supportive of the existing group status system. Subjects were identified as eight "intermediate grade" classrooms and teachers. The major finding of the study was that teachers in classrooms with good social climate did tend to be more supportive of the existing group status system than teachers in classrooms with poor social climates. This finding was qualified by the researchers, who noted that teachers in classrooms identified as having good social climate were significantly more learner-supportive in their total contacts with all students than were teachers in classrooms with poor climates (12).

The social status of the student may also be influenced by the teacher in relation to seating assignment. Being assigned a seat near the front of the class seems to indicate to others that the student is valued in a special way by the teacher. Schwebel and Cherlin found that being seated in the front of the classroom affected in a positive manner the way in which students are perceived by both their teachers and peers, as well as the way in which they evaluate themselves. The fifth-grade students in this study who were assigned seats in the front of the room received more sociometric choices from other students than did those seated in other positions (20).

Yet another teacher influence upon peer opinion is the teacher's use of "approval-focused desists," (I don't like students who waste time), or "task-focused desists," (If you continue to talk, you won't finish your project) with students. In a study by Rice, 23 eighth-grade male students and 32 eighth-grade female students were assigned to either an approval-focused or a task-focused treatment group. "Both the target and the teacher of the approval-focused desists were rated as having less desirable personality traits than when task-forced desists were used." (14).

A study by Engle, which was intended to explore the relationship between peer influences and achievement, provided instead some information about the relationship between peer contact in the classroom and attendance patterns. Engle's study was a three-year longitudinal one involving 440 seventh-, ninth-, and tenth-grade underachievers in groups which received either contact with peer leaders, personal counseling interviews, group counseling sessions, or "warm, sincere, interesting teachers," to determine which of the four interventions might improve academic performance.

None of the groups showed increased academic performance. However, members of groups which received contact with peer leaders and which were involved in group counseling sessions showed fewer absences and less tardiness, and "...milder, less frequent disciplinary problems." The suggested relationship between contact with peer leaders and reduced absenteeism is of interest, since very few studies have been undertaken to identify the relationship between quantity or quality of peer interaction within the classroom and attendance patterns among normal early adolescent students in the 11-to-13-age range (4).

Reynolds reported that a "Buddy System" was effective in promoting an understanding of the importance of good attendance among middle school and junior high school students (13).

A project undertaken by the Cedar Rapids, Iowa, and Iowa City Schools developed a 50-item questionnaire to gather information on junior high school student and teacher perceptions of factors relating to non-attendance. Survey results indicated that most student and teacher respondents believed truancy to be highly related to peer influence. While generally in agreement on the causes of truancy, students and teachers differed on solutions. Teachers favored increased structure, while students favored a more open environment (16).

Structured interviews with truants were used by Nielson and Gerber in a study of truancy among junior high school students (grades six to eight). These researchers identified and described two model types of truant students at grade levels six to eight. For those described as "authority defying" truants, the crucial school issues related most to school adults. Individuals in this group reported disagreements with teachers which they viewed unresolved "months after the problem had been referred to the assistant principal; challenges to school rules they felt unreasonable; and having difficulty thinking of anyone they admired at school." These students viewed the school as the major cause of their truancy. A second group of truants was termed "peer phobic." These students described few, if any, close peer relationships. When asked what they disliked about school and why they were truant, they all spoke of anxiety and embarrassment in encounters with peers (11).

A consensus of peer opinion regarding a student's level of performance may support or impede that student's involvement within the class, both academically and socially (17). Rosenholtz and Rosenholtz noted that group consensus regarding an indivudual's ability level is affected by the number of dimensions on which performance is evaluated, and by the visibility or publicness of that performance or evaluation (17).

In addition to organizational characteristics, the formation of peer opinion may also be influenced by the degree to which the teacher holds low expectations for a given student and communicates those low expectations to class members. Brophy and Good have identified several means by which teachers communicate low expectations of a student to both the student himself and to his classmates. In interacting with students for whom they hold low, rather than high, expectations, teachers tend to a) provide less time for students to respond; b) give the answer or call upon another student rather than rephrase the question; c) criticize proportionately more frequently when wrong answers are provided by the student; and, d) interact privately rather than publicly to a proportionately higher degree, which may be perceived by peers as a sign of inadequacy on the part of the student (2).

The middle school teacher who desires to support positive relationships to the peer group for individual students may be well advised to identify those students for whom low expectations are held, examine the interaction patterns that take place between themselves and such students, and consider the possible influence of these interaction patterns upon classroom peer group opinion of individual students.

REFERENCES

1. Ahlbrand, William P., Verbal participation and peer status, *Psychology in the School,* 1979, 7:247-249.
2. Brophy, Jere E., and Thomas L. Good, *Teacher-Student Relationships,* New York: Holt, Rinehart and Winston, Inc., 330-32.
3. Buswell, Margaret M., Relationship between the social structure of the classroom and academic success of pupils, *Journal of Experimental Education,* 1953, 22:37-52.
4. Engle, Kenneth B., A demonstration study of significant others in producing change in self-concept and achievement in Kalamazoo secondary school underachieves. A study undertaken by the Kalamazoo Board of Education, Kalamazoo, Michigan, 1965.
5. Hallinan, Maureen T., Structural effects on children's friendships and cliques, *Social Psychology Quarterly,* 1979, 42:43-54.
6. Hollander, E., and J. Marcia, Parental determinants of peer orientation and self-orientation among preadolescents, *Developmental Psychology,* 1970. 2:292-302.
7. Lippitt, R. and M. Gold, Classroom social structure as a mental health problem, *Journal of Social Issues,* 1959, 15:40-49.
8. Ludwig, D.J., and M.L. Maehr, Changes in self-concept and stated behavioral preferences, *Child Development,* 1967, 453-467.
9. Moreno, Jacob, *Who Will Survive?* Washington, D.C.: Nervous and Mental Disease Publishing Company, 1934.
10. Mozdoerz, G., M. McConville, and H. Krauss, Classroom status and perceived performance, *Journal of Social Science,* 1968, 75:185-190.
11. Nielsen, Arthur, and Dan Gerber, Psychosocial aspects of truancy in early adolescence, *Adolescence,* 1979, 14:313-326.
12. Polansky, Lucy, Group social climates and the teacher's supportiveness of group status systems, *Journal of Educational Psychology,* 1954, 28:115-123.
13. Reynolds, Carol, Buddy system improves attendance, *Elementary School Guidance and Counseling,* 1977, 11:305-306.
14. Rice, William, The effects of task-focused and approval-focused discipline techniques. Paper presented at the Annual Meeting of the American Educational Research Association, Washington, D.C., April, 1975.
15. Richardson, Steven, and others, Cultural uniformity in reaction to physical disabilities, *American Sociological Review, 1961, 26:241-247.*
16. Robinson, John, and others, Project probe: a student conducted truancy, Cedar Rapids, Iowa, and Iowa City Schools, 1979.
17. Rosenholtz, Susan, and Steven Rosenholts, Classroom organization and the perception of ability, *Sociology of Education, 54:132-140.*
18. Schiffler, N., J. Sauer, and L. Nadelman, Relationship between self-concept and classroom behavior in two informal elementary classrooms, *Journal of Educational Psychology,* 1977, 69:349-359.
19. Schmuck, R., Sociometric status and utilization of academic abilities, *Merill-Palmer Quarterly,* 1962, 8:165-172.
20. Schwehel, A., and D. Cherline, Physical and social distancing in teacher-pupil relationships, *Journal of Educational Psychology,* 63:543-550.

21. Sones, G., and Norma Feshback, Sex differences in adolescent reactions toward newcomers, *Developmental Psychology,* 1971, 381-386.
22. Torrance, E. Paul, Developmental changes in sources of consensual validation in preadolescence, *Gifted Child Quarterly,* 1971, 15:3-11.
23. Werdelin, Ingvor, A study of the relationshbip between teacher ratings, peer ratings, and self-ratings of behavior in school, *Scandinavian Journal of Educational Research,* 1969, 13:147-196.
24. Withall, John, An objective measurement of a teacher's classroom interactions, *Journal of Educational Psychology,* 1956, 47:203-212.
25. Whitmore, Joanne, The modification of undesirable attitudes and classroom behavior through constructive use of social power in the school peer culture, Technical Report No. 36, California: Stanford Center for Research and Development in Teaching, 1973.

May, 1982

5. Ability Grouping

Grouping students on the basis of measured or perceived ability is a very common educational practice. In fact, it has been estimated that more than 77 percent of the school districts in the United States use ability grouping (Findley and Bryan). Teachers generally believe that grouping students by ability is done fairly, is instructionally effective, makes teaching students at all ability levels easier, results in fewer discipline problems, and generates a better spirit of cooperation among students (Wilson and Schmits). However, they are uncertain if research findings support these beliefs about the effectiveness of ability grouping in schools.

This column reviews the relationships between ability grouping in schools and four other variables: teacher expectations of students, instructional procedures employed, students' perceptions of self and others, and students' academic achievement.

Ability grouping is defined as the selection or classification of students for schools, classes, or other educational programs based on differences in ability or achievement (ERIC). Initial grouping is done very early in a child's school career — usually in kindergarten or first grade. These early groupings are frequently based upon information from registration forms and parent interviews and can result in children being grouped according to the teacher's perception of the student's politeness, passivity, and the ability to listen and to follow directions. Such groupings, which likely reflect the family's socioeconomic status more than the child's ability or potential to learn, result in higher socioeconomic status children receiving favored treatment — more frequent and more positive interactions with teachers (Rist, 1970). Higher socioeconomic status is translated into "higher ability group" and results in selected students feeling superior to other students. Differences, initiated in kindergarten or first grade, are enhanced through second and third grades where higher status children stay together as an elite group which tends to remain fixed and rigid, **regardless of the children's performance.** When working with high ability groups, teachers tend to be concerned mostly about instructing the children; when working with low ability groups, teachers tend to be more concerned about controlling and disciplining students (Rist, 1970 and Mackler, 1966). These groups of students frequently move through their elementary and middle school experience intact. There is relatively little change in the assigned ability group after the third grade.

Teacher Expectations and Ability Groups

Students tend to perform better when teachers have high expectations of them and worse when teachers' expectations are lower (Rosenthal and Jacobson, 1968). Flowers (1966) used fictitious ability groupings to learn about the effects of teacher expectancy on pupil performance and teacher perceptions. His study was conducted in two different junior high schools located in two different cities. At the conclusion of the study, Flowers asked each teacher of the various courses in which the students were enrolled to answer a number of questions about the students. Compared to teachers of the control groups, teachers of the allegedly superior groups (1) referred more often to what the children could do rather than what they could not do, (2) found virtually no discipline problems in class, although discipline problems were reported by almost all teachers of control group children,

(3) referred more often to efforts to motivate their pupils and less often to the inadequacy of teaching materials, and (4) preferred teaching the "higher" ability group.

Several studies reviewed by Brophy and Good (1974) found that teachers over-react to grouping labels so that their teaching is not appropriately matched to student ability levels. In particular, teachers working with low ability level students in tracked schools tend to have inappropriately low expectations. Students in the lower tracks have been found to fall increasingly behind students of equal ability who were placed in higher tracks. Ability grouping apparently minimizes the achievement of students placed in the high track and the achievement of those placed in low tracks. Furthermore, once students have been placed in a particular ability group, teachers tend to "teach to the group" rather than to individuals within the group and teachers' expectations for the group undoubtedly influence the instructional procedures used.

Instructional Procedures and Ability Groups

Several studies have compared the instructional procedures used with high ability groups to those used with low ability groups. Stern and Shavelson (1981) reported an ethnographic study designed to learn how teachers' judgments of student abilities influenced the way fifth and sixth grade students were grouped for reading and the effect of these grouping practices on teacher planning and instructional behaviors. They concluded that students were grouped according to reading ability and, once grouped, the group and not the individual child became the unit for many teaching decisions. Plans for the low ability group differed considerably from those for the high ability group. With low ability students, teachers emphasized decoding and basic comprehension skills and gave highly structured assignments, while flexibility in procedures and assignments and emphasis on sophisticated comprehension skills were stressed for high ability groups. Eder (1982) examined the nature and extent of differences in the learning environments of high and low ability groups and also found that less able students were generally assigned to less stimulating groups. Martin and Evertson (1980) agreed that teachers used a more direct, less flexible approach with lower ability students. They found, however, that even though students in lower ability groups answered more questions incorrectly than their peers in the higher ability group, teachers praised them more often. Teachers were apparently satisfied to elicit any response from students in the low ability group regardless of the "correctness" of the response.

Evertson, Sanford, and Emmer (1981) reported that excessive heterogeneity of students' entering achievement levels in junior high English classes limits teachers' successful adaptation of instruction to individual student needs. When the range of students' abilities was greater, these researchers found a lesser degree of student engagement and cooperation. Teachers who were effective classroom managers adapted more easily to a wide range of student abilities than those who lacked management skills. However, they found no relationship between students' academic achievement and the heterogeneity of the classes.

In a study of peer influence on student attentiveness during classroom lessons, Eder (1982) found that students assigned to lower ability groups became inattentive more frequently than those assigned to higher ability groups. She found that one student's behavior often had a distracting effect on several peers simultaneously. Verbal behaviors were more distracting than nonverbal behaviors. These findings suggest that students placed in a lower ability groups are more likely to be distracted by a peer and to therefore have less opportunity to learn than their classmates in higher ability groups. Wilkinson, Cherry, and Calculator (1982) also reported peer-related advantages for students placed in higher ability groups.

Student Perceptions and Ability Groups

Student perceptions of self and others are affected by the ability group to which they are assigned. In general, students in higher ability groups are viewed more positively than those in lower ability groups regardless of academic achievement (Fagen, 1980; Schwarzwald and Cohen, 1982; Bayer, 1981; and Cotton and Savard, 1981). Based upon his study of sixth grade students, Levinson (1979) concluded that, "ability grouping leads to stereo-typed and stratified roles, and parental, teacher, and peer pressures that could prevent the student from developing healthy social relations and a positive self concept." Levinson also claimed it is possible that students in low groups may incorporate the teachers' judgment of their current status and ability and begin to behave according to these expectations.

These findings, coupled with the previously reported studies that indicated a strong relationship between ability group and socioeconomic status, suggest that the practice of grouping students by perceived ability may result in the development of deflated positive perceptions among lower socioeconomic level students. Furthermore, this effect would hold if a given student were assessing his own standing or that of a classmate, a situation which could systematically accentuate social class distinctions (Brophy and Good 1974).

Student Achievement and Ability Grouping

In spite of the lowered teacher expectations, less effective teaching strategies, and artificially altered student perceptions of self and others associated with ability grouping, the practice might still be defended if it results in improved academic achievement by all or most students. Unfortunately, research has never supported the idea that homogeneous grouping by ability improves student achievement (Wilson and Schmits, 1978). In a survey of more than 2,000 secondary schools, Doe (1978) found that basic skills in reading and math are just as good in schools using heterogeneous groups as in those using homogeneous grups. Other researchers whose findings indicate that ability grouping does not result in improved academic performance are Findley and Bryan (1971) and Holderman (1976). When the achievement of students in different ability groups is examined, the general conclusion is that students in the high ability group benefit from the practice and those in the low ability group suffer (Brophy and Good, 1974; Webb, 1980; Kulik, 1981; and Cotton and Savard, 1981). Generally, the gain by students in the high ability group is not as great as the loss by low ability grouped students.

Kulik (1981) reported that the positive effects of ability grouping were more dramatic when the teacher adjusted the instruction to match the ability level of students. While it seems quite reasonable to assume that such adjustments would be made, the literature suggests that teachers frequently do not alter their plans or lessons for students by ability apparently misleads teachers into believing that they do not need to attend to individual differences with the ability groups.

Summary

The practice of grouping students by ability for instructional purposes is not supported by research. Even though a majority of teachers believe that ability grouping improves the effectiveness of schooling, the studies reviewed suggest that the practice has deleterious effects on teacher expectations and instructional practices (especially for lower ability grouped students), student perceptions of self and others, and academic performance of lower abilitiy students. It interferes with opportunities for students to learn from — and learn to accept — peers of different socioeconomic backgrounds, and may perpetuate notions of superior and inferior classes of citizens. The practice is especially antithetical to the goals and objectives of the middle-school.

REFERENCES

Battle, M. Error reduction by freshman writers and its relationship to grouping. ERIC ED 188170, 1980.

Boyer, A social status for hierarchy: reading groups. *Viewpoints In Teaching and Learning*, 57:3, 49,-57, Summer, 1981.

Brophy, J.E. and Good, T.L. *Teacher-Student Relationships: Causes and Consequences*, Holt Rinehart and Winston, Inc., New York, 1974.

Cotton, K. and Savard, W. Instructional grouping: ability grouping. Research on School Effectiveness Project: Topic Summary Report, Northwest Regional Educational Lab, Portland, OR, May 1981, ERIC, ED 214704.

Dar, Y. and Rish, N., Homogeneity and heterogeneity in education. ERIC, ED 220543, 1981.

Doe, B. Mixed ability shines in tests. *Times Educational Supplement*, 3307:3, November 17, 1978 cited in Kirk, L., 1982.

Eder, D. Peer influence on student attentiveness during classroom lessons. Paper presented at the 66th Annual Meeting of the American Educational Research Association, New York, 1982.

Eder, D., Ability grouping as a self-fulfilling prophecy: a microanalysis of teacher-student interaction. *Sociology of Education*, 54:3, 151-162, July, 1982.

ERIC, Thesaurus of ERIC Descriptors 9th Edition, Onyx Press, Phoenix, AZ., 1982.

Everton, E., Sanford J. and Emmer, E. Effects of class heterogeneity in junior high school. *American Educational Research Journal*, 18:2, 219-232, Summer, 1981.

Fagan. M.J. Self concept and academic achievement: their relationship within and between streamed classes. *Humanist Educator*, 19:2, 91-96, December, 1980.

Findley, W. and Bryan, M., *Ability Grouping: 1970*, Athens, GA: Center for Educational Improvement, 1971.

Findley W. and Bryan M., *The Pros and Cons of Ability Grouping*, Phi Delta Kappan Educational Foundation, Bloomington, IN, 1975.

Flowers, E.C., Effects of an arbitrary accelerated group placement on the tested academic achievement of educationally disadvantaged students. Unpublished doctoral dissertation, Teachers College, Columbia University, 1966. Reported in Rosenthal and Jacobson, 1968.

Getzels, J., and Dillon, J. The nature of giftedness and the education of the gifted. In *Second Handbook of Research of Teaching*, Robert M. Travers, Editor, Rand McNally College Publishing Company, 1973, P. 689 ff.

Grant L., and Rothenberg, J. Charting educational futures: interaction patterns in first and second grade reading groups. Paper presented at the Annual meeting of the American Educational Research Association, Los Angeles, CA., 1981, ERIC ED 200902.

Holderman, K., Ability grouping — its effect on learners. *NASSP Bulletin*, 60: 85-89, February, 1976.

Haller, E., Davis, S., Does socioeconomic status bias the assignment of elementary school students to reading groups. *American Educational Research Journal*, 17:4, 409-418, Winter, 1980.

Kirk, C., Effects of ability grouping on secondary school students. Paper presented at the annual meeting of the American Educational Research Association, Los Angeles, CA., 1981. ERIC ED 204417.

Kulick, C., Effects of ability grouping on secondary school students. Paper presented at the annual meeting of the American Educational Research Association, Los Angeles, CA., 1981. ERIC ED 204417.

Levenson, S. Ability grouping in schools: a national phenomena. ERIC ED 182823, 1979.

Mackler, B., Grouping in the ghetto. *Education and Urban Society*, 2:80-96, 1969, cited in Brophy and Good, 1974.

Martin, J. and Evertson, C., Teachers' interactions with reading groups of differing ability levels. University of Texas, Austin, Research and Development Center for Teacher Education, 1980.

Oakes, J. Tracking policies and practices; school by school summaries. *A Study of Schooling in the United States*. Technical Report Series, No. 25, California University, Los Angeles, 1981, ERIC ED 214893.

Rist, R., Student social class and teacher expectations: the self-fulfilling prophecy in ghetto education. *Harvard Educational Review*, 40: 411-451, 1970.

Rosenthal R. and Jacobson, L., *Pygmalion in the Classroom*, Holt, Rinehart and Winston, Inc., New York, 1968.

Schwartzwald, J. and Cohen, S. Relationship between academic tracking and the degree of interethnic acceptance, *Journal of Educational Psychology*, 74:4, 588-597, August, 1982.

Stern, P., and Shavelson, R. The relationship between teachers grouping decisions and instructional behaviors: an ethnographic study of reading instruction. Paper presented at the annual meeting of the American Educational Research Association, Los Angeles CA., 1981, ERIC ED 201971.

Webb, N.M., An analysis of group interaction and mathematical errors in heterogeneous ability groups. *British Journal of Educational Psychology*, 50:3, 266-276, November, 1980.

Wilkson, L., Cherry L., and Calculator, S., Requests and responses in peer-directed reading. *American Educational Research Journal*, 19:1, 107-120, Spring, 1982.

Wilson, B.J. and Schmits, D.W. What's new in ability grouping? *Phi Delta Kappan*, 59:8, 535-536, April, 1978.

August, 1983

6. Diagnostic Prescriptive Teaching

Diagnostic prescriptive teaching is defined as the "process of diagnosing student abilities, needs, and objectives and prescribing requisite learning activities." (19). Scolon claimed that this approach uses a rational analysis of available information on each student, allows the teacher to pinpoint the nature of learning deficiencies, and give strong clues about experiences that will correct deficiencies (15). The mode is supported by many educators and at least one state requires that all preservice teachers be trained in its use (17). However, the model is not universally acclaimed. After an extensive review of research on its use with special education, Arter and Jenkins recommended that diagnostic-prescriptive teaching be discontinued (1).

These divergent recommendations are due in part to the student characteristics that are diagnosed and serve as a basis for prescribed instruction. Arter and Jenkins reviewed the model in terms of general psychological processes that may underlay academic learning. These processes include auditory discrimination, visual discrimination, auditory and visual memory, cross sensory perceptual abilities and psycholinguistic abilities as measured by tests such as the Illinois Tests Of Psycholinguistic Abilities and the Development Test of Visual Perception. The natures of the prescriptions were consistent with the skills diagnosed; attention was given to remediating deficiencies in general psychological processes or to using instructional approaches that capitalized upon general psychological process strengths of the student. The Peabody Language Development Kit and the Frostig Program for the Development of Visual Perception were cited as examples of instructional materials used to develop general psychological processes. Based upon their review of research specific to special education, Arter and Jenkins concluded that:

1. Tests used for the diagnosis of general psychological processes are not reliable;
2. The tests used lack concurrent validity with respect to academic achievement, predictive validity for academic performance, diagnostic validity, and construct validity;
3. General psychological process are highly resistant to training by existing programs; and
4. Attempts to use these diagnostic test results to prescribe instructional approaches that capitalize on student strengths have not resulted in better academic performance.

Hence, they recommended a moratorium on advocacy of the differential diagnostic-prescriptive teaching model, on classification and placement of children according to differential ability tests, on the purchase of instructional materials and programs which claim to improve these abilities, and on course-work to train differential diagnostic-prescriptive teachers (1).

However, Arter and Jenkins were careful to distinguish the diagnosis of specific behavioral components and prerequisite skills related to objectives in a learning hierachy. Most supporters of the diagnostic-prescriptive teaching model recommend using it with specific educational objectives (12). Each student's competence relative to the objectives should be assessed and appropriate instruction prescribed on the basis of the diagnosis.

Yeany, Dost and Matthews listed six steps to follow when using the diagnostic prescriptive approach in this manner (21).
1. The instructor defines expectations in terms of student post-instruction outcomes (i.e., instructional objectives).
2. Test items are prepared that correspond to the instructional objectives.
3. Instruction is planned and carried out to help students achieve the objectives. Any materials may be used and any appropriate teaching procedures may be followed.
4. Diagnostic tests related to the objectives are given either before or after instruction or both. The tests are short and are given frequently so that learning problems are quickly identified.
5. Students are provided feedback on how they performed on the diagnostic tests. Remedial work is prescribed for students who do not achieve an objective.
6. Additional cycles of instruction-diagnostic testing-remediation may be carried out with either individuals or groups (conditions may preclude taking all students to mastery.)

Yeany, Dost and Matthews compared the achievement of students who received only instructional objectives with that of students receiving objectives, diagnostic test results and recommended remedial activities. The students in this study were preservice elementary teachers enrolled in a biology course. Students were administered an achievement test upon completion of a unit. Comparisons of test performance indicated that students who received objectives, diagnostic test results, and recommended remedial activities scored significantly higher on fact recall items than did students who received only instructional objectives (21). Other writers report facilitative effects of diagnostic-prescriptive teaching in reading (10,13), writing (9, 16), mathematics (6, 7, 20), and science (8, 11, 14, 21, 23).

The Saunders and Yeany study is particularly interesting because it is one of only a few that used a middle school population. They assessed the effect of diagnostive-prescriptive teaching on the immediate and retained achievement of middle school science students (14). Three intact groups of students were used. Each group experienced one of three treatments: no diagnosis or remediation; diagnosis with no remediation; or diagnosis and remediation. Immediate achievement was measured at two points during the experiment and retention was measured 30 days following the experimental unit. There were no significant differences among the three groups on the immediate tests. On the retention measure, however, the groups received diagnosis with and without remediation both outscored the group that received no diagnosis or remediation. Diagnostic testing accompanied by feedback on performance apparently improved the retention of information.

These results support Okey's recommendation that students be administered a diagnostic test, informed of the results of their tests and encouraged to study on their own. Any remedial work would be the student's responsibility.

Yeany and Miller reported the results of a meta-analysis on the effects of diagnostic-prescriptive science teaching which lends additional support to this truncated version of the model (23). Three comparisons were examined: comparisons between groups receiving diagnosis and remediation, only diagnosis, and neither diagnosis nor remediation. The researchers concluded that achievement can be significantly and positively influenced thorough diagnostic-prescriptive teaching. The magnitude of the influence can be expected to be about .55 standard deviation units of achievement when compared to an instructional strategy that does not use diagnosis and prescription. Further, they concluded that *the source of this impact does not appear to be the remediation but rather the diagnostic feedback.* The difference in scores between the groups receiving diagnosis and remediation and those receiving only remediation was not significant.

The positive effects of diagnostic-prescriptive teaching reported by researchers are supported by practitioners in the field. Reiff (13), Bloom and Hastings (2), Siegal (15), West (20), Dodd et al. (6), Cotham (4) and Dishner and Readence (5) reported positive effects and recommended specific approaches for implementing this approach.

Conclusions

The studies reviewed and current practices examined suggest that use of the diagnostic-prescriptive teaching model with specific instructional objectives will improve instruction in the middle school. Diagnosing student capabilities and prescribing learning activities relative to specific instructional objectives has been shown to facilitate learning. On the other hand, diagnosing underlying psychological processes and prescribing instruction to remediate deficiencies in areas such as auditory discrimination has been shown to be of limited value.

For science instruction, diagnostic feedback is as useful as feedback plus remediation when the diagnosis is specific to stated instructional objectives. In the absence of prescribed remedial activities, students seem able to attend to their own remediation provided they are informed of specific deficiencies. Additional research is needed to determine if this conclusion is valid for other academic areas.

REFERENCES

1. Arter, J.A. and J.R. Jenkins, Differential diagnosis-prescriptive teaching: a critical appraisal, *Review of Educational Research,* 49:517-555, fall, 1979.
2. Bloom, B.S., T. Hastings and G.F. Meadus, *Handbook of Formative and Summative Evaluation of Student Learning:* New York: McGraw-Hill, 1971.
3. Cooper, K., Diagnostic teaching, *Education 3-13,* 5:12-16 April, 1977.
4. Cotham, J., CAPPS and science: diagnostic/prescriptive instruction, *Hoosier Science Teachers,* 5:113-115, May, 1980.
5. Dishner, E.K. and J. Readence, Getting started: using the testbook diagnostically, *Reading World,* 17:36-39 October, 1977.
6. Dodd, C.A., G.A. Jones and C.E. Lamb, Diagnosis and remediation of pupil errors: an exploratory study, *School Science and Mathematics,* 75:270-276, March 1975.
7. Fowler, M.A., Why did he miss that problem? *Academic Therapy,* 14: 23-33, September, 1978.
8. Goodson, M.L. and J.R. Okey, The effects of diagnostic tests and help sessions on college science achievement, *Journal of College Science Teaching,* 8:89-90, 109, 1978.
9. Junkala, J., Task analysis, handwriting and process based instruction, *Journal of Learning Disabilities* 13: 49-53, January, 1980.
10. Laughter, M.Y., and L. Livengood, Will differeniation of instruction help middle school students achieve at levels higher than their expected pace? *Middle School Reserach Studies, 1980,* National Middle School Association, Fairborn, Ohio, 1980.
11. Okey, J.R. Altering teaching and pupil behavior with mastery teaching, *School Science and Mathematics,* 74:530-535, 1974.
12. Orlich, D.C. and others, *Teaching Strategies A Guide to Better Instruction,* Lexington, Mass., D.C. Heath and Company, 1980, pp.75ff.
13. Reiff, J., Improving reading instruction through diagnosing, *Reading Improvement,* 15: 40-42, September, 1978.
14. Saunders, R.L. and R.H. Yeany, Diagnosis, remediations and locus of control: effects on immediate and retained achievement and attitudes, Paper presented at the annual meeting of the National Association for Research in Science Teaching, Boston, Mass., April, 1980.

15. Sconlon, Robert. Diagnostic-prescriptive teaching, progress and problems, Paper presented at AACTE 30th Annual meeting, Chicago, Illinois, February 22, 1978, ERIC publication ED 179538.
16. Siegal, D., Who said Johnny can't write? *American Education*, 15: 4, 27-32, May, 1979.
17. *Standards for Colleges or Universities Preparing Teachers*, Ohio Department of Education, Columbus, Ohio, 1975, p.4.
18. Strange, M. and R.L. Allington, Use the diagnostic prescriptive model knowledgably, *Reading Teacher*, 31: 290-293, December, 1977.
19. *Thesaurus of Eric Descriptors*, Oryx Press, Phoenix, Arizona, 1980.
20. West, T.A., Rx for verbal problems; a diagnostic-prescriptive approach, *Arithmetic Teacher* 25: 57-58, November, 1977.
21. Yeany, R.H., R.J. Dost and R.W. Matthews, The effects of diagnostic-prescriptive instruction and locus of control on the achievement and attitudes of university students, *Journal of Research in Science Teaching*, 17:537-545, November, 1980.
22. Yeany, R.H. and P.A. Miller, The effects of diagnostic/remedial instruction on science learning: a meta-analysis, Paper presented at the annual meeting of the National Association for Research in Science Teaching, Boston, MA, April, 1980.
23. Yeany, R.H., M.J. Waugh, and A.L. Blalack, The effects of achievement diagnosis with feedback on the science achievement and attitude of university students, *Journal of Research in Science Teaching*, 16: 465-472, 1979.

August, 1981

7. Classroom Time

The way teachers use classroom time has drawn increasing attention from researchers. The reasons for this awakened interest among researchers parallel the reasons that practitioners have become interested in the topic. First, classroom time is a finite resource that must be allocated in accordance with the priorities of the teacher. Second, it is relatively easy to measure when compared with other, less precise concepts, such as motivation and attention. Finally, time-on-task is what Benjamin Bloom calls an "alterable variable," one that can be manipulated by the researcher, or, as in this case, the teacher (2).

Most important, though, is the fact that time on academic task has been linked, clearly and consistently, with student achievement. Even very general variations in academic time expenditure appear to be related to achievement. For example, the length of the school day reported by teachers correlated positively with a variety of achievement measures in reading and mathematics, as did average daily school attendance (9, 18). It comes as no surprise to teachers or administrators that pupil and teacher absence correlates negatively with achievement in those same areas (3, 9, 10).

More specific research studies have produced results that are quite similar to the attendance studies. Stallings and Koskowitz (17) found that time devoted to mathematics and reading, as well as time children spent with academic texts, yielded significant and consistent positive correlations with academic achievement. Other research supports this conclusion, suggesting that the amount of time allocated for student exposure to academic material is related to student performance, even when the effects of individual teacher, student attributes and school setting are controlled (8, 12).

Perhaps even more significant than these positive relationships is the finding that *no* non-academic activity has correlated positively with student achievement, and that many time-expending behaviors show a *negative* correlation with achievement in academic subjects. Activities such as group time, active play, child selection of seating and work groups are negatively correlated with student achievement measures among primary children (17). Because these types of activities are so central to middle school programs, it is important to replicate the time and achievement studies at the middle school level as well, recognizing that not all of the middle school's objectives are academic achievement oriented.

Effective teachers appear to spend a significant portion of their time on academic tasks such as talking about the subject, asking questions, answering questions, correcting subject-related student responses, or supervising independent learning activities by her pupils (11). Increasing achievement in reading appeared to bear a strong relationship to the percentage of time teachers invested in these behaviors, with the most effective teachers spending about eighty-eight percent of their time thus engaged (11).

Also enlightening are studies that report how classroom time tends to be spent. Calfee and Hoover-Calfee (5) found that time expenditure seemed to be a function of grade level and subject. Reading and language instruction was more likely to proceed directly, with the teacher retaining control over the activity, whereas mathematics instruction was more likely to be achieved through independent student work overseen and monitored by the teacher. They found also that most class time was spent practicing skills. Relatively little time was spent on new ideas and topics, but at the fifth grade level a substantial amount of time was spent applying skills and knowledge to problems outside of the school context. Nevertheless, most classroom time was spent doing seatwork, more so in the upper elementary grades than in the primary grades. Discussions and recitations occurred about twenty percent of the time.

We cannot infer from all of these findngs, however, that simply increasing the amount of time spent on learning tasks will produce a commensurate increase in achievement. Some evidence exists that the relationship between time and achievement may be curvelinear (12, 13), that is, operating on a principle of "dimishing returns." After a certain "most-efficacious" amount, additional time expenditure may produce no additional learning or may actually impede learning. Part of this relationship may be explained by the fact that teachers provide relatively more resources (time, attention) to lower achieving students and less with more capable students (13). While this may be due, in part, to a teacher giving fewer minutes of high quality time to brighter students, it may also be that a characteristic of more capable students is their ability to manage their own academic time more effectively.

Other variables may affect the relationship between time and achievement as well. The socio-economic status of the school, interacting with the nature of the assignment given, appeared to produce different effects of achievement. In low socio-economic status classrooms, time spent on individually prescribed work or on seatwork was correlated positively with achievement. Time spent on oral response, discussion and recitation, however, was negatively related to achievement. In high socio-economic status classrooms, the opposite was true: time spent on oral responding was related to achievement in a positive fashion (4). Other evidence suggests that the nature of the academic content and the general ambiance of the classroom setting also affect the time-achievement relationship in significant ways (15). Disagreement also exists over whether direct or indirect instruction is the most effective way of increasing time on task (15, 5), although some of the interaction effects noted in a variety of studies suggest that the most effective method may be a function of the content and the ability of the student.

Among the most interesting findings are those suggesting that differences in student ability may be found in differences between the elapsed time allotted to a task and the amount of time the student is actively *engaged* in the task. More able students, it seems, spend more allotted time "on-task," engaged in behavior relevant to the task at hand (1). A model suggested by Carroll (6) proposes that learning is a function of the amount of time given to a learning situation in relation to the time needed by the learner to complete the task (6, 16, 14). Combining these findings, we can hypothesize that more effective schools are those which allow different amounts of time to be spent on a task, depending upon the amount of time needed by each individual student, and which act to reduce the amount of time that a student spends "off-task."

The relationship between time on task and student achievement appears to be consistent and reasonable. Caution must be exercised, though, so that irrelevant tasks are not created simply to fill time. In the middle school setting it is especially important to recognize that not all of the school's objectives are academic achievement related. By attending to developmental concerns in the physical, social and emotional areas we may actually create an environment in which the student can spend more time "on-task" because other, more fundamental, needs have been satisfied. The use of classroom time is a complex issue, but it is clear that time which is not spent on purposeful activity is likely to produce little academic achievement.

REFERENCES

1. Anderson, Lorin W. An empirical investigation of individual differences in time to learn, *Journal of Educational Psychology*, 68:226-233, 1975.
2. Bloom, Benjamin S. The new direction in educational research, *Phi Delta Kappan*, 61:382-385, February, 1980.
3. Bond, Guy L. & Robert Dykstra. The cooperative research program in first-grade reading instruction, *Reading, Research Quarterly*, 2:1-42, Summer, 1967.
4. Brophy, Jere E. and C.M. Evertson, *Process-Product Correlations in the Texas Teacher Effectiveness Study: A Final Report*, Austin: University of Texas, 1974.
5. Calfee, Robert & Hoover-Calfee, Cathryn. Reading mathematics observation system, description & measurement of time usage in the classroom, *Journal of Teacher Education*, 4:323-325, Winter, 1976.
6. Carroll, John B. A model of school learning, *Teachers College Record*, 64:723-733, May, 1963.
7. Corno, Lyn. Classroom management on the manner of time, in Duke (ed.) *Classroom Management*, Seventy-eighth Yearbook of NSSE, Chicago: University of Chicago Press, 1979.
8. Good, Thomas L. and D.A. Grouws. Teaching effectiveness in fourth grade mathematics classrooms, in Borish, G. *The Appraisal of Teaching*, Reading, Mass.: Addison-Wesley, 1977.
9. Harris, Arthur J. et al., *A Continuation of the CRAFT Project: Comparing Reading Approaches With Disadvantaged Negro Children* in Primary Grades. U.S. Office of Education Project 5-0570-1-12-1; New York: Teacher Education Division, CCNY, 1968, (ERIC: Ed 101 297).
10. Harris, Arthur J. & B.L. Sewer. Comparison of Reading Approaches in *First Grade Teaching With Disadvantaged Children*, U.S. Office of Education Project 2677; New York: City University of New York, 1966.
11. Hautala, Lynda W. & Aaron, Robert L. Time use: a variable in teacher effectiveness. Paper presented at the Annual Meeting of the National Reading Conference. (27th New Orleans, LA) December, 1977.
12. Kidder, Steve, et al. Quantity and quality of instruction: empirical investigation, Paper presented at the Annual Meeting of the American Educational Research Association, Washington, D.C. March 31-April 3, 1975. (ERIC: Ed 110 471).
13. Kiesling, Herbert. Productivity of instructional time by mode of instruction for students at varying levels of reading skill, *Reading Research Quarterly*, XIII:554-581, 1977-78.
14. Rodgers, Frederick, Influence of time variations on learning and achievement, *Educational Leadership*, 101-105, October, 1969.
15. Rosenshine, Barak. Classroom instruction in Gage (ed.) *The Psychology of Teaching Methods*, the Seventy-fifth Yearbook of the NSSE, Chicago: University of Chicago Press, 1976.
16. Sjogren, Douglas. Achievement as a function of study time," *American Educational Research Journal*, 4:337-343, November, 1967.
17. Stallings, Jane & David Kaskowitz. *Follow-Through Classroom Observation Evaluation*, 1972-73, Menlo Park, California: Stanford Research Institute, 1974.
18. Wiley, David E. & Annegrette Harnischfeger. Explosion of a myth: quality of schooling and exposure to instruction, major educational vehicles, *Educational Researcher*, 3:7-12, April, 1974.

August, 1980

8. Developing Problem Solving Skills

Teaching students to use school-learned information to solve real life problems is a widely accepted educational goal. Champagne and Klopfer (4) summarized the history of problem solving as a goal of science education, the entire 1980 Yearbook of the National Council of Teachers and Mathematics was devoted to the subject (13), and the writers for the disciplines of social studies (28), economics (27), communications (5), and engineering (14) continue to advocate problem solving skills as desirable instructional outcomes. Nevertheless, the judgment of parents and teachers, supported by the results of national assessments, suggests that schools have failed to achieve this goal.

Teaching problem solving skills is hampered by the absence of a clear understanding of what "problem solving" is (4) and how it should be taught (4,9). Research on problem solving is difficult to conceptualize because of the lack of a general theory in the area of human problem solving (9).

This report of research indicates the difficulty of defining problem solving as a skill and describes the work of James Greeno (9) which attempted to develop a theory of human problem solving and to use that theory as a framework for reviewing the experimental psychology of problem solving. It also identifies the classroom variables that have been found to facilitate or interfere with problem solving and recommends instructional practices that should contribute to developing student problem solving skills.

What do we mean by "problem solving"? Champagne and Klopfer (4) explicitly stated that "there is no single source, nor a simple combination of several sources, to which one can turn for a functional account of the behaviors, skills, or competencies that constitute the ability to solve problems." This absence of a detailed description or definition of problem solving has been blamed for the school's failure to develop problem-solving skills. If the product is undefined, how are we to recognize it or plan instruction to achieve it? Attempts to define "problem solving" as an educational outcome are derived from two sources: educational philosophy and current research. John Dewey, a seminal writer who published extensively from 1884 to 1948, advocated a curriculum based on problems. He defined a problem as anything that gives rise to doubt or uncertainty. Problem solving is the process by which one removes this doubt or uncertainty. His definition of a problem is similar to the operational definition found in the 1980 *Thesaurus of ERIC Descriptors.* There, problems are defined as "difficulties or obstacles not easily overcome." It is interesting to note that the *Thesaurus* does not report an operational definition for "problem solving."

James Greeno, a researcher who has published numerous articles on this topic, proposed that our understanding of problem-solving could be improved by categorizing problems according to the psychological processes used to solve them. The skills and knowledge needed to solve a given problem can then be identified and instructional practices to develop the required skills can be planned. He listed three types of problems, gave examples of each, and identified the skills and knowledge required to solve each type. (See Figure 1) Greeno acknowledged that most real life problems are a combination of his problem types - that is, real life problems are likely to require inducing structure with transformations, or transformations of arrangements, or generation of structure and arrangement. The task of using Greeno's typology to classify subject related problems which students are asked to solve and of determining if students actually use the psychological processes and skills he hypothesized remains to be done.

FIGURE 1
GREENO'S TYPOLOGY OF PROBLEMS

TYPE OF PROBLEM & CHARACTERISTICS	EXAMPLE	SKILLS OR KNOWLEDGE REQUIRED TO SOLVE
1. **Inducing Structure** Some elements are given and the main task is to identify the pattern of relations present.	Analogies like Boy:Man::Girl:?	Requires skills to identify relations among "components" and fitting the relations into a pattern — these are the main processes involved in "understanding." Requires skills in planning.
2. **Transformation** An initial situation, a goal, a set of operations that produce changes in situations are given and the task is to find a sequence of operations that transforms the initial situation into the goal.	Puzzles like the Tower of Hanoi, where a stack of different size disks must be moved around one disk at a time, with no disk ever placed on a peg that already holds a smaller disk. The task is to move a stack of disks from one peg to another. Anograms like TUDSETNS which require the problem solver to form a word from the letters.	
3. **Arrangement** The problem solver is presented with some "elements" and is required to arrange them in such a way that a given criterion is satisfied.		Requires skills in composition, a process of constructive search where the problem solver must find the solution in a search space and must also be able to generate the possibilities that constitute the search space.

The meaning of problem-solving may be clarified somewhat by listing the procedures recommended to solve problems (13). First, the problems must be understood. What is the goal? What information is available? What constraints apply? Second, a plan for solving the problem must be developed. Several strategies for moving from the initial situation to the goal are available and one or more of these needs to be chosen. Third, carry out the plan. Check to assure that each step was correct. Fourth, examine the solution. Does the result make sense? When students are able to use these procedures for the purpose of overcoming difficulties or obstacles related to a specific subject area, they will have mastered problem-solving in that subject area.

The probability that students will develop effective problem-solving skills depends upon the classroom climate and instructional practices used by the teacher.

Research suggests that cooperative classrooms in which students are encouraged to express their ideas contribute to the development of problem-solving skills. The advantage of a cooperative classroom climate over a competitive or individualistic one was supported by Johnson, Skon and Johnson (11). They found that students who cooperated with one another during instruction were more likely to develop effective problem solving skills and strategies than those who worked independently or who competed with one another. Creative problem-solving is also more probable when there is a strong emphasis on developing an accepting attitude toward novel ideas and unusual insights (9-24). This is probably related to the students' willingness to consider and propose different problem solutions. Experiments have shown that individuals will increase their use of uncommon responses when they are encouraged to do so (9).

In addition to establishing an appropriate classroom climate, teachers can contribute to the development of problem-solving skills by using learning activities that require students to solve problems, by integrating new content information with the students' existing knowledge, by selecting problems that are interesting and relevant to the student, and by discussing problem solving strategies with students and suggesting alternative approaches for solving problems.

The need to engage students in problem solving activities in order to teach the process is self-evident. Russell and Chiapetta (20) found that eighth grade science students who engaged in problem-solving laboratory activities developed better problem solving skills than those who experienced laboratory lessons that simply confirmed earth science concepts. The positive influence of a problem oriented instructional approach on problem solving skills is supported by others (5,21,22).

Helping students relate new information to their existing knowledge is a frequently overlooked approach when developing problem solving skills. Mayer (17) found that the ability to solve problems depends upon the amount of information the student is given, the student's existing relevant knowledge, and which aspects of the student's existing knowledge are activated during learning and integrated with the new material. The benefit of making students aware of the relationship between new and previously learned information is also supported by Ausubel's theory of advanced organizers.

Students are more likely to attend to, engage in, and reflect upon problems that are interesting and relevant to them (12, 18). Examples of interesting problems that may be modified to make them relevant to students were easily found in the areas of math (16,12), science (12,18,19), and social studies (25,28). Similar problems could probably be found or developed for other subjects.

Once a problem has been solved, students should discuss the approach they used and compare it with other approaches. While there are usually several ways to solve a problem, one approach is likely to be more efficient than another. If students develop the habit of using the same problem solving approach all the time, they are likely to encounter problems that they cannot solve and/or use a round-about approach when a more direct solution is available (9). There are several problem solving strategies such as trial and error, working forwards, working backwards, using analogies and others with which the student should become familiar (13,29).

Several writers have extracted recommended classroom practices from the research on problem solving (3,7,22,23). Two of these will be reported here because they seem to incorporate the major research findings and apply to all subject areas. Flener recommended that teachers
1. whenever possible, embed a teaching/learning experience in a problem solving format.

2. think in terms of hints or suggestions rather than absolute procedures to be followed.
3. experiment by giving students less help than usual.
4. not be misled by the immediate benefits of teaching by telling - the long range benefits of teaching through problem solving may be higher.(7)

Forty years ago, Brownell developed the following list of suggestions for teachers which is still appropriate.
1. To be most fruitful, practice in problem solving should not consist of repeated experiences in solving the same problems with the same techniques, but should consist of the solution of different problems by the same techniques and the application of different techniques to the same problems.
2. A problem is not necessarily 'solved' because the correct response has been made. A problem is not truly solved unless the learner understands what he/she has done and knows why his/her actions were appropriate.
3. Instead of being 'protected' from error, the child should many times be exposed to error and be encouraged to detect and to demonstrate what is wrong and why.(7)

Teachers, administrators and parents apparently value problem solving skills as an outcome of school instruction. Unless specific attention is given to developing these skills, it is unlikely that students will develop the desired competence necessary to solve the real-life problems they encounter.

REFERENCES

1. Bass, Lawrence, S. Problem-solving science. *Instructor*, 90(9):93, 96, 98, April, 1981.
2. Beane, James A. The general education we need. *Educational Leadership*, 37:307-08, Jan. 1980.
3. Brownell, William. Problem solving *The Psychology of Learning*, 41st yearbook of the NSSE, pt. 2, Chicago: The Society, 1942 cited by Suydam (23).
4. Champagne, Audrey and Klopfer, Leopol. Problem solving as outcome and method in science teaching: insights from 60 years experience. *School Science and Mathematics* 81 (1), 3-8, Jan., 1981.
5. Christians, Clifford. Problem solving in a mass media course. *Communications Education*, 28 (2): 139-43, May, 1979.
6. DeVault, M. Doing mathematics is problem solving. *Arithmetic Teacher*, 28(8): 40-43, April, 1981.
7. Flener, Frederick. Reflections on problem solving study. *International Journal of Mathematics Education in Science and Technology*, 9:9-13, Feb., 1973, 1978 cited by Suydam (23).
8. Friessen, Charles. Problem solving: meeting the needs of the mathetically gifted students. *School Science and Mathematics*, 80:127-30, Feb., 1980.
9. Greeno, James G. Nature of problem-solving abilities in *Handbook of Learning and Cognitive Processes*, edited by W.K. Estes, Hillsdale, N.J.: LEA Publishers, 1978.
10. Grouws, Douglas A. and Thomas, William E. Problemsolving: a panoramic approach. *School Science and Mathematics*, 81:307-14, April, 1981.
11. Johnson, David W. and others. Effects of cooperative, competative, and individualistic conditions on children's problem solving performance. *American Education Research Journal*, 17:83-89, Sp. 1980.
12. Krockover, Gerald H. Solving everyday problems by applying science and mathematics principles. *School Science and Mathematics*, 79.607-612, Nov., 1979.
13. Krulik, Steven and Reys, Robert, Editors. *Problem Solving in School Mathematics* 1980 Yearbook, National Council of Teachers of Mathematics, Reston, VA, 1980.
14. Larking, Jill H. Processing information for effective problem solving. *Engineering Education*, 70:285-288.
15. Maline, Jane T. Strategies in mathematical problem solving. *Journal of Educational Research*, 73:101-108, Nov.-Dec., 1979.

16. May, Lola and Bethel, Barbara. Problem solving. *Instructor*, 90(9):54-55, April, 1981.
17. Mayer, R.E. Information processing variables in learning to solve problems. *Review of Educational Research*, 1975, 45:525-541.
18. Mettes, C.T. and others. Teaching and learning problem solving in science. Part I: A General Strategy. *Journal of Chemical Education*, 57:882-85, Dec. 1980.
19. Metes, C.T. and others. Teaching and learning problem solving in science. Part II: Learning Problem Solving in a Thermodynamics Class. *Journal of Chemical Education*, 58:51-55, Jan., 1981.
20. Russell, J. Michael and Chiapetta, Eugene. The effects of a problem solving strategy on the achievement of earth science students. *Journal for Research in Science Teaching*, 18:295-301, July, 1981.
21. Sage, James E. Problem solving performances: teaching methods make a difference. *Journal of Studies in Technical Careers*, 1:113-118, Winter, 1979.
22. Schoenfield, Alan H. Teaching problem solving skills. *American Mathematical Monthly*. 87 (10): 794-805, Dec., 1980.
23. Suydam, Marilyn. Untangling clues from research on problem solving in *Problem Solving in School Mathematics*. Krulik S. and Rays, R., Editors, Reston, Va.: National Council of Teachers of Mathematics, 1980.
24. Torrance, E.P. *Encouraging Creativity in the Classroom*, Dubuque, Iowa: Brown, 1970. cited by Greeno (9).
25. Turner, Thomas N. Question games for social studies. *Social Education* 45:194-196, March 1981.
26. Van de Walle, John and Thompson, Charles S. Fitting problem solving into every classroom. *School Science and Mathematics*, 81:289-97, April, 1981.
27. Walstad, William. Economic problem solving for the classroom. *School Science and Mathematics*, 81:289-97, April, 1981.
28. Weiss, Steve; Kinney, Mark; and others. Problem solving in social studies. *Social Studies*, 71:244-249, Nov.-Dec., 1980.
29. Wickelgren, W. *How to Solve Problems*. San Francisco: Freeman, 1974.

November, 1981

9. Critical Thinking*

Critical thinking is listed as one of the most important skills teachers needed to teach students (PAR Newsletter, 1980; Siegel, 1977 & 1980; Swick & Miller, 1975; Scheffler, 1973; Skinner, 1971; Follman and Lowe, 1972; Gantt, 1970; Woods and Walton, 1974; Follman, Brown & Burg, 1970; Anderson, Marcham & Dunn, 1944). Skinner (1971) states critical thinking is important because it helps students learn how to deal with rapid societal change, put new knowledge to use and make decisions. Brown and Brown (1971) and Woods and Walton (1974) discuss the importance of critical thinking as a method students can use to avoid believing educational misconceptions and to deal more effectively with social concerns (Anderson, Marcham & Dunn, 1944). Siegel (1980) states that critical thinking is important because it emphasizes mutual respect for ideas and the equal moral worth of teachers and students. He also states that this type of thinking teaches students necessary skills for a productive life, independence in learning, and encourages an accurate evaluation of ideas.

In reviewing the literature, Woods and Walton (1974) and Henderson (1972) and Gray (1969) found that critical thinking is thought of as an important educational goal, but is not taught extensively. They suggest that critical thinking is not being taught because the majority of teachers are unprepared to teach it well.

There has been little consensus in the literature about the definition of critical thinking. Ennis (1962) and Henderson (1972) define critical thinking as the "correct assessing of statements." Rust, Jones and Kaiser (1972) and Brown and Brown (1971) define critical thinking as the mental ability to use past experience and knowledge to accurately evaluate and assess the manner in which conclusions are reached. Siegel (1980) states that critical thinking is the ability to accurately evaluate statements, understand their importance and comprehend reasons for the stated conclusions.

Others have divided critical thinking into major components to try to better understand the concept. Follman, Brown and Burg (1970) cited recognition of assumptions, judgments of conclusions, and fine discrimination about the accuracy of inferences as the three major components of critical thinking. In Rust, Jones and Kaiser's (1962) study, the three major components of critical thinking were general reasoning, logical discrimination, and application of ideas and semantics. Follman and Lowe (1972) conducted a study to enhance critical reading and thinking in 5th and 12th graders. They found that students with a strong language ability scored high on measures of critical thinking. In reviewing the literature, Henderson (1972) found that the two major components of critical thinking are understanding the meanings of words in relation to the situation and determining if the conclusion that follows the information is appropriate. Skinner (1976) lists the process components found in the literature that are most frequently associated with critical thinking. They are the ability to recognize a problem, formulate an hypothesis, test the hypothesis, gather data, analyze data, reject or accept the hypothesis, and draw conclusions. Madison (1971) reviewed several definitions of critical thinking and concludes that critical thinking is a generic term encompassing both process and ability components. An operational definition of critical

*Dr. Christina K. McCann helped in preparing this review of research.

thinking that includes both the process and ability components derived from the literature is offered by Siegel (1980) as the ability to accurately evaluate statements and to understand their importance and relation to the stated conclusions.

Educators have been concerned about what type of student can learn critical thinking skills and what effect such learning has on student achievement. Gray (1969) and Saadeh (1969) reviewed the literature on critical thinking and discussed several important factors related to this concern. They found that the ability to think critically can be taught effectively to people two years of age and older. It was also found that I.Q. level was not related to the ability of a student to think critically. Gray (1969) and Saadeh (1969) also found that when students were taught critical thinking skills, significant achievement gains were reported in grades 1-6. They conclude from these findings that critical thinking can be taught in all subjects and grade levels.

Anderson, Marcham and Dunn (1944) conducted an experimental critical thinking program in 7th grade geography and 10th grade world history. Their results suggest that this program greatly improved the students' ability to accurately draw inferences and conclusions.

Smith (1960) concludes in his review of the literature that little progress has been made in distinguishing among the most effective materials and methods to teach critical thinking because the majority of studies have not assessed teacher differences. He suggests that teachers need to better understand classifying, explaining, conditional inferring, comparing and contrasting, valuating and designating. Smith thinks if the teacher understands these processes and can teach the students the appropriate logical operation, they will be able to improve critical thinking skills in students.

Saadeh (1969) also found that the research implied that no one method is best in promoting critical thinking. However, evidence showed critical thinking could be taught by involving and challenging the student. Siegel (1980) recognizes a "critical spirit" in students who continually seek evidence and reasons and are predisposed to understand ideas. He states that if a teacher can understand and apply critical thinking influences to educational content and the manner of teaching, the "critical spirit" can be reinforced.

More specific teaching methods that promote critical thinking are found in the literature. Siegel (1980) refers to a method that allows the student to ask questions and demand reasons and honesty from teachers. In this method teachers' ideas are evaluated by the student, a procedure which reinforces critical thinking.

Skinner (1976) suggests that teachers ask students questions that have many answers, force students to think, and allow the student time to practice critical thinking. He found critical thinking does not increase with age, only with practice.

Brown and Brown (1971) suggest a method of teaching critical thinking in middle school science after students have a firm grasp of the topic. The method includes an overview of the concept, a comfortable learning atmosphere where the students feel free to question and explore ideas with the teacher, practice of critical thinking skills and the development of a need in students to question and solve problems. Brown and Brown (1971) cite studies which indicate that creating the need in students to question and solve problems can be achieved quite easily.

Another method recommended in the PAR Newsletter (1980) is a four step process to facilitate critical thinking. First, the teacher identifies transferable thinking skills. Next, the teacher picks the appropriate activities that promote critical thinking. The teacher then describes how he/she want the students to grow. Finally, activities are provided for this growth.

Analogy, according to Swick and Miller (1975) is the best method to teach critical thinking. They describe four types of analogies found to be effective. These are justification through elaboration, illustration by the use of slang phrases, cause and effect, and fantasy-fact relationships.

Another method of teaching critical thinking is discussed by Gantt (1970). This method trains the teachers to decode student cues and respond to student needs through questioning. The questioning technique includes rephrasing, assisting pupils in gathering data resources, analyzing information, identifying examples and drawing out student experiences.

Hanf (1971) suggests the method of mapping to help students learn how to think critically. Mapping helps students receive, organize and evaluate information so it makes sense to them. The map becomes a graphic display of the main points and key words that present the identification of the main idea, subcategories and supporting details.

Another teaching method that can produce critical thinking is simulation gaming (Hyman, 1974). Hyman states that students can practice critical thinking through analysis, decision making, and the socialization that is endemic in the games.

The discovery through discussion method as described by Hyman (1974) has also been found to promote critical thinking. The steps include students deriving data from the topic without the assistance of the teacher. The students generalize the information and draw inferences about the data. The main role of the teacher is one of facilitator, helping students locate reference material and keeping the discussions on track.

The Taba Model of teaching is also recommended to promote critical thinking (Eggen, Kauchak and Harder, 1979). The seven phases of the Taba Model include listing data on a topic, grouping data, labeling categories, analyzing data, generalizing data, explaining inferences and generalizations, and application of generalizations.

The Suchman Inquiry Model is also promoted as a method to develop critical thinking in students (Eggen, Kauchak & Harder, 1979). The steps in this model include identifying a problem, suggesting appropriate solutions, gathering data, revising solutions and repeating the last two steps until all information is systematically evaluated.

The major indicators of critical thinking found in the literature can be used as a comprehensive checklist to assess both teaching methods and materials (Scheffler, 1973 & Siegel, 1980). Ennis' (1962) list of criteria for assessing teaching methods and teaching materials provide a reasonable summary of these indicators:
1. Grasping the meaning of a statement.
2. Judging whether there is ambiguity in a line of reasoning.
3. Judging whether certain statements contradict each other.
4. Judging whether a conclusion follows necessarily.
5. Judging whether a statement is specific enough.
6. Judging whether a statement is actually the application of a certain principle.
7. Judging whether an observation statement is reliable.

8. Judging whether an inductive conclusion is warranted.
9. Judging whether the problem has been identified.
10. Judging whether something is an assumption.
11. Judging whether a definition is adequate.
12. Judging whether a statement made by an alleged authority is acceptable.

Materials and methods which promote these cognitive activities may be judged to enhance critical thinking among students.

Cox (1970) suggests three other criteria for assessing materials used for critical thinking. The material should provide a stimulus for critical thought, present a question to be solved and supply sufficient information to the student. A more comprehensive checklist for assessing materials that are designed for critical thinking follows:

1. The material teaches the student to follow the evidence and accurately make fine discriminations about the truth or falsity of inferences.
2. The material teaches the student how to understand linguistic expressions.
3. The material teaches the student how to use and construct an advance organizer.
4. The material teaches the student how to judge conclusions.
5. The material teaches the student how to reason.
6. The material teaches the student how to discriminate.
7. The material teaches the student how to apply ideas.
8. The material teaches the student how to draw conclusions.
9. The material teaches the student how to make decisions.
10. The material involves and challenges the student.
11. The material develops in the student a need to explore and question. (The "critical spirit").
12. The material provides practice of critical thinking skills.

If the major indicators cited for the teaching of critical thinking and the assessment of materials promoting critical thinking are applied, critical thinking can be taught and enhanced in educational settings. Presumably, the promotion of these skills are especially important for middle school youth who are developing new mental and verbal capacities and new ways of viewing and evaluating their world.

REFERENCES

Anderson, H., Marcham, F. & Dunn, S., An experiment in teaching certain skills of critical thinking. *Journal of Educational Research*, 1944, 38:4:241-251.

Brown, S., & Brown, L. Suggested thinking and inquiry techniques in science for middle school teachers, *School Science and Mathematics*, 1971, 71:8:731-736.

Cox, D., Criteria for evaluation of reading materials, *The Reading Teacher*, 1970, 24:2:140-145.

Eggen, P., Kauchak, D., & Harder, R., *Strategies for Teachers*, Prentice Hall, Englewood Cliffs, N.J., 1979.

Ennis, R., A concept of critical thinking, *Harvard Educational Review*, 1962, 32:1.

Follman, J., Brown, L., & Burg, E., Factor analysis of critical thinking, logical reasoning and english subtests, *The Journal of Experimental Education*, Summer 1970, 38:4:11-16.

Follman, J. & Lowe, A., Empirical examination of critical thinking-overview, *Journal of Reading Behavior*, Summer 1972, 73, 5:3:159-168.

Gantt, W., Questioning for thinking: a teaching strategy that makes a difference for disadvantaged learners, *The Reading Teacher*, October 1970, 24:1:12-16.

Gray, M., Research and elementary school critical reading instruction, *The Reading Teacher*, February 1969, 22:5:453-459.

Hanf, M., Mapping: a technique for translating reading into thinking, *Journal of Reading*, January 1971, 225-230.

Henderson, K., The teaching of critical thinking, *Educational Forum*, November 1972, 37:1:45-52.

Hyman, R., *Ways of Teaching*, (2nd ed.), J.B. Lippincott, Philadelphia, PA, 1974.

Madison, J., Critical thinking in the classroom, *English Journal,* November 1971, 60:8:1133-1140.
Practical Applications of Research, Newsletter of Phi Delta Kappa, Center on Evaluation, Development and Research, Bloomington, Indiana, 3:1, September 1980.
Rust, V., Jones, R., Kaiser, H., A factor-analytic study of critical thinking, *The Journal of Educational Research,* March 1962, 55:6:233-259.
Saadeh, I., The teacher and the development of critical thinking, *Journal of Research and Development,* Fall 1969, 3:1.
Scheffler, I., *Reason and Teaching,* The Bobbs-Merril Company Inc., Indianapolis, Indiana, 1973.
Skinner, S.B., Cognitive development: a prerequisite for critical thinking, *The Clearing House,* March 1976, 49:292-299.
Skinner, S.B., The myth of teaching for critical thinking, *The Clearing House,* February 1971, 45:372-375.
Smith, B., Critical thinking, American Association of College Teacher Educators 13th Annual Meeting, 1960.
Swick, K., & Miller, H., Utilization of analogies to teach critical thinking skills, *The Clearing House,* December 1975, 48:180-182.
Woods, J., & Walton, D., Informal logic and critical thinking, *Education,* 1974, 95:1:84-86.

February, 1982

10. Attitude Development

The middle school years comprise a time of rapid physical and emotional change, and a time when students' attitudes toward themselves, others, school and various subjects begin to become more stable. An important function of the teacher is to assist students in developing attitudes that enable them to function as responsible members of society. However, such assistance may be difficult to give for two reasons.

First, teachers may not know the kinds of attitudes which will be most beneficial to the student. The decision of which attitudes to develop may be influenced by the values espoused by the teacher, parents, community, or some outside agency. When these values conflict with one another, the teacher may be in a situation where it is safer to ignore the development of attitudes and concentrate on academic matters. Since attitude formation and alteration is inevitable, inattention to attitude development will not result in more stable attitudes, but in a haphazard pattern of development that is likely to produce a contradictory and dissatisfying attitudinal set. Middle school teachers need to have a clear perception of their role in the development of student attitudes if they are to provide youngsters significant help with this important task.

A second cause of teacher failure to provide adequate guidance in the development of attitudes is that teachers often do not know how to intervene systematically in the change of student attitudes. Social psychology and educational research provide useful suggestions for developing desired attitudinal changes among middle school students.

Mager (6) defined attitude as a general tendency of an individual to act in a certain way under certain conditions. He described an attitude as a predisposition to approach or avoid a given object, event or idea. A positive attitude is reflected by the student's tendency to initiate contact with the attitudinal object while a negative attitude is demonstrated by the tendency to avoid contact whenever possible. If this definition is accepted, we can infer a student's attitude toward math, for example, by observing how frequently the student chooses to talk about math, read books related to math, and so forth. A student exhibiting a greater number of these behaviors probably has a more positive attitude toward math than one exhibiting fewer approach tendencies.

Wagner (10) provided a more precise description of attitudes. He stated that attitudes are composed of cognitive, affective and behavioral components which correspond to what we believe about, how we feel about and how we act toward the object of the attitude. It is not necessarily true that beliefs, feelings and actions are consistent. Wicker (12) reviewed 46 studies of relationships between verbal and behavioral responses and concluded that expressed beliefs and feelings are only slightly related to one's behavior.

The relationship between student performance in a given school subject and stated beliefs and feelings about that subject is also only moderate. A student who likes math, for example, may receive lower math grades than one who dislikes it. Mager (6) suggested, however, that attitudes toward school subjects will affect subsequent behaviors toward those subjects. That is, a middle school student who has a negative attitude towards math may do well in the subject but never apply his or her knowledge when the course is over. Students with positive attitudes will have a greater tendency to use what they've learned and to engage in math-related activity later in their lives. Since the purpose of schooling is to help students function better in society — ie., to use what they know — *developing positive attitudes toward school subjects is equal in importance to teaching subject-related information and skills.*

Approaches to Developing Deisred Attitudes

Attitude formation and change is possible in schools because attitudes are learned (13). Children are not born liking or disliking specific school subjects, nor do they enter the world with positive or negative self concepts. Such attitudes are the result of learning experiences in the home, community and school. While some attitudes are firmly established by the time students enter the middle school, it is nevertheless true that middle school teachers can have a profound effect on student attitudes. Systematically or unwittingly, teachers influence student attitudes through classical conditioning, operant conditioning and modeling.

Positive attitudes are developed through *classical conditioning* when an initially neutral or negative object is paired with one that elicits a positive reaction. The conditioning is completed when the neutral object begins to elicit a positive reaction on its own. Pavlov (8), teaching his dog to salivate at the sound of a bell, is the traditional example of classical conditioning. The same approach is effective when developing attitudes. (4, 5). Students who interact with one another in pleasant surroundings are more likely to develop positive interpersonal relationships than those interacting in less pleasant surroundings. Classical conditioning theory suggests that associating specific subjects with favorable learning experiences will result in more positive attitudes toward the subject. Part of the task of developing positive attitudes toward school subjects can be accomplished by using enjoyable activities to teach the subject's content. Such activities might include small group activities where students work with well-liked peers, field trips or other out-of-the-ordinary instructional activities, additional hands-on learning experiences, or some form of student selected activity.

In a similar manner, teachers can unwittingly develop negative attitudes toward school or specific school subjects by pairing learning experiences with aversive conditions. For example, the student who is embarrassed by group showers may learn to dislike physical education if the association between showers and that particular subject is strong enough. Students may also develop negative attitudes toward a specific skill, such as writing, as a result of being required to practice the skill under unpleasant circumstances. Students who are given writing assignments as punishment for misbehavior or who are forced to write about dull topics will soon learn to avoid writing. The frequently heard complaint that school instruction is "not relevant to my needs" may explain some negative student attitudes toward school.

Operant learning theory is based upon the assumption that behavior is controlled by its consequences (9). According to this theory, students are more likely to develop attitudes that result in postive reinforcements than they are to adopt attitudes that result in punishment. Mager (6) described several techniques which teachers can use to apply operant learning theory.

The first step in applying the theory is to recognize an approach tendency toward school when it occurs. Behaviors such as saying positive things about school, engaging in school activities, or attending school on a regular basis may exemplify approach tendencies. Next, the teacher must reinforce the desired attitude or positive approach tendency when it occurs. Unfortunately, teachers frequently use ineffective reinforcers, those that are not valued by the students. Ware (11) found that students prefer personal types of recognition to tangible prizes and that many extrinsic rewards utilized by schools, such as trophies and trips, were not highly regarded by students. Assuming that the teacher is using an appropriate reinforcer, the desired attitude needs to be initially reinforced on a regular basis; after the attitude has been demonstrated by the student on several occasions, the reinforcer may be removed gradually. The approach is analogous to contingency management and/or behavior modification.

A third approach to developing desired attitudes in middle school students is *modeling* (3). Many student attitudes are formed by observing the response of others to the object or event in question. If a teacher appears to enjoy the subject being taught and to be *really* interested in class discussions, students are likely to develop more positive attitudes toward the subject. Bandura's (2) findings suggest that students are more likely to imitate a model who has prestige in the eyes of the students and are more likely to adopt attitudes that have been observed to result in reinforcement rather than punishment. Teachers need to be especially careful *not* to model undesirable attitudes. They must also be aware that the attitudes modeled and reinforced by a student's peers may exert a great influence on the attitudes developed by that student. This suggests that teachers should pay special attention to the attitudes expressed by peer group leaders, the ones whose attitudes are most likely to be emulated by the rest of the class.

A different approach to changing student attitudes toward specific objects and events is suggested by *dissonance theory* (7). The basic assumption underlying dissonance theory is that an individual strives for consistency among his beliefs, opinions, attitudes and behavior. The theory suggests that awareness of inconsistencies causes the individual to become psychologically uncomfortable; an aversive state results and the individual will strive to reduce the inconsistency. The dissonance may be reduced by changing existing opinions, beliefs or attitudes.

Assume, for example, that a middle school student believes that science is an unimportant subject and that his negative attitudes toward science are demonstrated by the effort he exerts to avoid the subject. The student would not experience dissonance because his beliefs, attitudes and actions are consistent. If, however, the student could be convinced that scientific achievements have enabled man to survive and that additional scientific knowledge would lead to solutions to many problems facing today's society, his new beliefs would be inconsistent with negative attitudes toward science. The student would experience dissonance which could be reduced by a positive shift in his attitudes toward science. The greater the inconsistency, the greater the attitude change predicted by dissonance theory.

Several techniques have been found to be effective in producing dissonance. A straightforward approach is to present, through a respected source, information that is inconsistent with current beliefs. The resulting conflict between beliefs may result in desired attitudinal changes.

A second approach is to have students role play a situation which requires behaviors that are inconsistent with their current attitudes (1). For example, a student could role play a character defending the need for compulsory education.

If behaviors engaged in during the role-playing situation were inconsistent with the student's current attitudes, he might experience dissonance. Since he could not change the fact that he behaved as he did, the student may develop more positive attitudes toward compulsory education.

Other techniques for generating dissonance are to have students debate a position with which they disagree, write a paper supporting a previously unacceptable position or present an oral report defending a desired attitudinal position which the student previously opposed. In each case, the teacher places the student in a situation that is likely to cause dissonance among existing beliefs, opinions and attitudes. The student may reduce the dissonance by shifting his attitudes in the desired direction.

Student attitudes do change and may stabilize during the middle school years. The changes may be desirable or they may result in attitudes that are inconsistent with educational goals. By systematically applying attitude change techniques, the chances of developing desirable attitudes among middle school students can be improved.

REFERENCES

1. Barron, R.A., D. Byrne, and W. Graffitt. *Social Psychology*. Boston, Massachusetts: Allyn and Bacon, Inc., 1974.
2. Bandura, A. Social learning through imitation, in M.R. Jones (ed.) *Nebraska Symposium on Motivation*. Lincoln, Nebraska: University of Nebraska Press, 1962.
3. Bandura, A. *Psychological Modeling*. Chicago: Aldene-Atherton, 1971.
4. Graffitt, W. Environmental effects on interpersonal behavior: ambient effective temperature and attraction. *Journal of Personality and Social Psychology*, 1970, 15:240-244.
5. Graffitt, W. and R. Veitch. Hot and crowded: influence of population density and temperature on interpersonal affective behavior. *Journal of Personality and Social Psychology*, 1971, 17: 92-98.
6. Mager, Robert F. *Developing Attitude Toward Learning*. Belmont, California: Fearon Publishers, 1968.
7. Mayo, C. and M. LaFrance. *Evaluating Research In Social Psychology*. Monterey, California: Brooks/Cole Publishing Company, 1977.
8. Pavlov, I.P. *Conditioned Reflexes*. London: Oxford University Press, 1927.
9. Skinner, B.F. *Science and Human Behavior*. New York: Macmillan, 1953.
10. Wagner, Richard V. The study of attitude change: an introduction, in *The Study of Attitude Change* edited by Richard Wagner and John Sherwood. Belmont, California: Brooks/Cole Publishing Company, 1969.
11. Ware, B.A. What rewards do students want? *Phi Delta Kappan*, 1978, 59: 355-356.
12. Wicker, A.W. Attitudes versus actions: the relationship of verbal and overt behavioral responses to attitudinal objects. *Journal of Social Issues*, 1969, 25: 41-78.
13. Zembardo, P.G., E.B. Ebbesen and C. Maslack. *Influencing Attitudes and Changing Behaviors*. Reading, Massachusetts: Addison-Wesley Publishing Company, 1977.

November, 1979

11. The Teacher's Effect on Pupil Self-Concept and Related School Performance — Part I

It is established in both the theory and folklore of education that teachers have a significant effect on the self-concepts of their pupils. Branan (1972) provides empirical confirmation of this belief by reporting that college students who were asked to describe their most negative experiences almost always listed personal interactions, the large majority of which were with teachers. Incidents such as humiliation in front of the class, embarrassment, unfairness and damage to self confidence placed teachers far ahead of the next most significant group, parents, in their capacity to influence student self-concept.

Among middle school educators, the study of teacher effects on self-concept is especially important, not so much because of the empirical evidence which points to the relationship between a healthy self-concept and student adjustment and achievement, but because the development of a positive self-concept is itself a central objective in many middle school programs. Most ot the contemporary writers in the area of middle school curriculum advocate, as a high priority, attention to the development and enhancement of pupil self-concept (Eichhorn, 1966; Lounsbury and Vars, 1978; Overly, Kinghorn and Preston, 1972).

Among the most fundamental parts of a pupil's self-concept that the teacher can effect is the student's development of a body image or a picture of "physical self." Adams and Cohen (1974) found that, in primary classrooms, students rated low in facial attractiveness received more supportive and neutral teacher contacts than those rated above average. In seventh grade classrooms, this pattern did not occur, indicating a shift in teacher concerns from facilitating pupil adjustment to school to task achievement. In Clifford's (1975) intriguing study, teachers were given photos of and simulated performance information on a group of first grade pupils and asked to estimate a number of variables related to pupil success, achievement and relationship with peers. The attractiveness of the pupils had a significant effect on teacher estimates of pupil IQ, parental interest in the student's achievement and probable level of education. Attractiveness had no effect on teacher estimates of pupil self-concept or success in peer relations. In other words, while the teachers were influenced by student appearance in making judgments about their children, they did not think that their students were likely to allow attractiveness to influence their interpersonal relationships.

Related to the development of body image is the teacher's reaction to handicapped students, an especially important issue because of the potential modeling effect a teacher may have in a "mainstreamed" classroom. Teachers who do not "believe in" the consequences of a handicap and those who overreact in order to project a nurturant image do little to help the child develop a realistic self-image with respect to the handicapping condition (Kash and Borich, 1978). Wolfgang and Wolfgang (1968) found that while teachers expressed very positive attitudes toward childrens' handicaps, the amount of social distance maintained by the teacher seemed to vary with the nature of the child's handicap. Teachers were closer to children with temporary handicaps, such as broken arms, than they were to children with chronic/uncontrollable handicaps, such as amputations.

Teachers maintained the greatest distance from children with chronic but controllable conditions such as obesity or decayed teeth.

Keeve (1967) found that schools sometimes perpetuate false body concepts and maladaptive behavior by treating temporary handicaps as chronic. Among students who were excused from physical education classes, Keeve found a number who were not handicapped in any way. Their excuses were based on past conditions or old diagnoses that no longer provided an accurate description of the child's physical condition. However, by continuing to modify the students' programs, the school was encouraging them to behave as if they were still handicapped.

Children develop perceptions of their bodies, and the advantages and disadvantages of their physique, in large measure from the ways they are called upon to use their bodies in the classroom (Kash and Borich, 1978). Short children stand in front rows; tall ones decorate the room and hold up display pieces. Heavy girls play the part of the grandmother, slender girls the mother. Small children are the mice/leaves/children/flowers/sheep; stocky boys move the scenery (Kash and Borich, 1978). To some degree, these events are logical outcomes of body type, and help children to build an accurate picture of their physical capacities. In other cases, the physical characteristics are used as a basis for restricting participation in certain activities which are not related, in any logical or reasonable way, to body type.

Walker (1962) found that teachers could predict how children were likely to behave on the basis of their body types. However, this may have been due, in part, to the way children were channeled into specific activities on the basis of how their physiques were perceived by teachers. For example, children who have minor speech impediments may not speak in class very often not because they are reluctant to do so, but because the teacher does not call upon those children for fear of embarrassing them. In another situation, a tall boy may be encouraged into a position on the basketball team, with all of its attendant social ramifications, simply because he is tall and not because of any love for the sport.

Apart from channeling, teacher expectations, both reasonable and unrealistic, have a significant effect on student self-concept. Most often, though, teachers' expectations are communicated to students in ways even the teacher is unaware of. For example, Good (1970) found that high achieving students were usually given more opportunity to speak than were low achievers. Brophy and Good (1970) reported that boys generally receive more direct questions and more praise for correct answers than do girls. At the same time, boys have more interaction with the teacher and are the object of more teacher criticism than are girls. Rubovits and Maehr (1973) found that high IQ black students received less attention overall than other students, and that more of that attention was negative or critical.

Among the most fascinating of all studies are those dealing with the extent to which student behavior fulfills teacher expectation...the so-called "self-fulfilling prophecy." Rist (1970) found that the ability groupings in primary classrooms paralleled the socio-economics status of the children in the classroom. In addition, the higher ability children were located closer to the teacher and were more often engaged in interaction with the teacher than were their lower ability peers. Because this pattern persisted throughout elementary school, Rist concluded that the teacher's expectations influenced student achievement and, thereby, affected the expectations of future teachers as well.

Although direct, casual relationships between teacher expectations and pupil performance have not been estabished, it is clear that teacher bias toward students can be altered (Meichenbaum, Bowers, and Ross, 1969; and Palardy, 1969) and that such alterations, usually produce changes, however inconsistent, in student performances. Clearly, though, the way teachers view pupils, and the extent to which they convey those perceptions are likely to have an effect on the pupils' self-concept and subsequent school performance.

A more detailed discussion of the ways in which pupil self-concept, subject as it is to alteration by the teacher, relates to pupil achievement and classroom behavior will be presented in the next column.

REFERENCES

Adams, G.R. and A.S. Cohen 1974. Children's physical and interpersonal characteristics that affect student-teacher interactions, *Journal of Experimental Education.* 43 (1): 1-5.

Branan, J. 1972. Negative human interaction. *Journal of Counseling Psychology.* 19(1): 81-82.

Brophy, J. and T. Good 1970. Teachers' communication of differential expectations for childrens' classroom performance: some behavorial data. *Journal of Educational Psychology.* 71: 365-374.

Claiborn, W.C. 1969. Expectancy effects in the classroom: a failure to replicate. *Journal of Educational Psychology.* 60: 377-383.

Clifford, M.M. 1975. *Physical attractiveness and academic performance.* Paper presented at annual conference of American Educational Research Association, Washington, D.C.

Eichhorn, D. *The middle school.* New York Center for Applied Research in Education, 1966.

Good, T. 1970. Which pupils do teachers call on? *Elementary School Journal* 70: 190-1980.

Kash, M.M. and G.G. Borich, *Teacher Behavior and Pupil Self-Concept.* Reading, Mass.: Addison-Wesley, 1970.

Keeve, P.J. 1967. Perpetuating phantom handicaps in school age children. *Exceptional Children.* 33(8): 539-544.

Lounsbury, J. and G. Vars. *A Curriculum for the middle school years.* New York: Harper and Row, 1978.

Meichenbaum, D.H., K. Bowers and R. Ross. 1969. A behavioral analysis of teacher expectancy effect. *Journal of Personality and Social Psychology* 13(4): 306-316.

Overly, D.E., J.R. Kinghorn and R.L. Preston. *The Middle School,* Worthington, OH: Charles A. Jones, 1972.

Palardy, J.M. 1969. What teachers believe — what children achieve. *Elementary School Journal.* 69(7): 370-374.

Rist, R.C. 1970. Student social class and teachers' expectations: the self-fulfilling prophecy in ghetto education. *Harvard Educational Review.* 40: 411-451.

Rubovits, P.C. and M.L. Maehr 1973. Pygmalion black and white. *Journal of Personality and Social Psychology.* 25(2): 210-218.

Walker, R.N. 1962. Body build and behavior of young children: I. Body build and nursery school teachers' ratings. *Society for Research in Child Development.* 27(3), Monograph No. 84.

Wolfgang, J. and A. Wolfgang 1968. *Personal space-an unobstructive measure of attitudes toward the physically handicapped.* Paper presented at the annual conference of the American Psychological Association, San Francisco.

February, 1981

12. Self-Concept and School Performance — Part II*

In the previous column, we examined the manner in which a teacher affects the self-concept of their students and, for the moment, ignored the question of what impact self-concept has on school performance. Although it takes only a cursory glance at curriculum, methods, administration or counseling literature to conclude that self-concept and its enhancement is a high priority consideration for the education professional, the reasons for this intense interest are somewhat elusive. Common sense seems to dictate that how students feel about themselves should influence how they perform school tasks and how they behave in the school environment. However, the correlations between general assessments of self-concept and wide-range measures of achievement and behavior have remained weak and inconclusive. Because the logic of the relationship remains convincing, the area has not been abandoned by researchers, and more clearly focused and refined studies have yielded important conclusions that substantiate the profession's interest in the enhancement of self-concept and the development of self-esteem.

There is a body of literature, albeit small, which suggests that a direct, linear relationship between self-concept and school achievement may exist. In a 1967 article, Bledsoe notes a strong relationship between children's self-concept and measures of academic achievement. Cappadona and Kerzner-Lipsky (1979) found a significant relationship between student self-concept, as measured by the Coopersmith Self-Esteem Inventory, and performance on a standardized mathematics achievement test. Brookover and his colleagues (1964) reported correlations of .42 and .39 between grade point average and self-concept for one thousand urban seventh graders. While this relationship is not strong, it is, nevertheless, statistically significant.

It is not *statistical* significance but *practical* significance that is important to practitioners, so we can probably conclude that it is not the weak relationship between achievement and self-concept that gives self-concept its importance to the school professional. The intuitive significance we attach to the student's self-concept results, no doubt, from a much stronger and more observable series of phenomena than what is suggested by the unimpressive correlation coefficients noted earlier. In order to trace this intuition, it is important to examine research which suggests the way that self-concept affects behaviors that are, themselves, related to academic achievement.

Rosenberg and Gaier (1977), for example, studied learning disabled and "normal" males in grades 7 and 8. They found that LD students found it difficult to talk in front of their peers and, therefore, did not like to be called upon in class. The learning disabled youngster also lacked tenacity, being much more easily discouraged than his "normal" counterpart. Although a negative relationship was found between the LD students' rather low self-concept and their academic performance, the study also suggests that self-concept affects other behaviors which contribute to achievement and, thereby, exerts an indirect but important influence on achievement in school.

Studying reading group membership in the first grade, Weinstein (1976) found that students in low reading groups have reduced status in the classroom and this

*H. Willis Means participated in the preparation of this review.

status is reinforced by the teacher, leading to the conception on the students' part that they are different from others in the room. The reminders of their status, when coupled with the need for stability that is common among lower self-esteem children, may contribute to reduced academic performance in reading.

In a similar study, Zimmerman and Allenbrand (1965) found that good readers (those performing well on reading achievement measures) could be characterized as better adjusted than the poor readers. They tended to set long-term goals and express more confidence in their ability to meet those goals than the poor readers, who avoided long range goals and did not view their own effort as being closely related to future events or conditions. Zimmerman concludes, "as compared to the poor reader, the good reader is more apt to describe himself as well-adjusted and motivated by internalized drives which results in effortful and presistent striving for success."

Stanwyck and Felker (1973) clarify this drive to act in accordance with our expectations of our own ability. In studying students in grades 3-6, they found that these students had a need for "self-consistency," a term which describes the equilibrium resulting from acting the way we expect ourselves to act. Low self-concept students enter a form of conflict whenever they succeed because it defies their own self-expectations. They can resolve this conflict either by adjusting their self-concept to accommodate the success, or by rejecting the success as meaningless or the task as trivial. In this study, low self-concept students tended to resolve this conflict in the latter fashion, an outcome which raises questions about the use of success-building as a method for enhancing self-concept.

Research by Coopersmith (1967) lends additional credence to the findings reported above. He found that people with high self-esteem approach tasks with the intent that they will succeed whereas low self-esteem people believe they will fail. People with low self-esteem may reject the success they have earned, and may go so far as to sabotage their own efforts. In their study of law school students, Curtis, Zanna and Campbell found that students with a low self-concept will actually act in ways that prevent the success they are capable of achieving in order to avoid the conflict that would result between self-expectation and successful performance. High self-concept students did not appear to exhibit either this conflict or the accompanying self-defeating behavior.

Liska (1975) identifies the way in which self-concept may affect behavior by pointing out that an individual will seek consistency. A student with a low self-concept is likely to continue to do the things that reinforce his image. This striving for consistency may take the form of disruptive behavior because the student is accustomed to negative comments from the teacher and his peers and does not want to experience the conflict and anxiety that would be produced by an alteration of his behavior patterns.

Just how dramatically self-concept can be related to behavior is illustrated in an article by Reckless and Dinitz (1967). Based on a longitudinal study of junior high school boys, the authors concluded that self-concept may have a direct bearing on the behaviors that are normally associated with juvenile delinquency. Boys with a positive self-concept were less likely to engage in behavior that would result in delinquency than those with a lower self-concept.

The most comprehensive and authoritative study of self-esteem was conducted by Stanley Coopersmith and his associates in 1967. At the conclusion of his eight year study of nearly eighteen hundred subjects, he was able to report findings that provide a most penetrating and provocative view of self-concept and the manner in which it relates to behaviors assocated with school performance in a wide variety of domains.

On three related variables, conformity, creativity and independence, Coopersmith found that high self-esteem subjects tended to resist social pressures to conform, relying on their own analysis of situations, and their own creative mechanisms to arrive at solutions to problems. The high esteem group was more likely to express its convictions on an issue, regardless of what they perceived the majority point-of-view to be. As can be expected, high self-esteem people are less concerned than low esteem people with criticisms that might be levied by their peers for behavior or opinions that are contrary to those of the majority. In this sense, they are more independent or "inner directed." They believe that they are responsible for what happens to them and are less accepting of fatalistic arguments about the future.

High and low self-esteem groups also differ in creative performance, with high esteem people demonstrating more creative behavior on a variety of measures. According to Coopersmith, these differences "are manifest across...different conceptual, linguistic and artistic skills," suggesting that "persons high in their own evaluation are generally more capable of achieving and imposing original solutions than persons who are less confident in themselves." Kash and Borich (1978) add that "creative behavior seems...closely linked to...(1) acceptance and approval of task-directed but non-conforming behavior, (2) acceptance of pupil ideas and exploration, (3) a basic attitude of trust that allows risk-taking, and (4) freedom within cultural sex roles."

Low self-esteem people, according to Coopersmith, are generally very aware of themselves in public situations, and very likely to be self-conscious. They tend to dwell on their own inadequacies, conjuring up a host of reasons for the inevitability of their failures. They tend to remind themselves of past failures and, by paralyzing themselves with feelings of insufficiency and vulnerability, reduce their chances for success in any public encounter.

Among Coopersmith's most important findings are those associated with the relationship between emotional states and self-concept. He reports that people with low self-esteem have "a more impoverished emotional life" than those with high self-esteem. They tend to be more anxious and demonstrate symptoms of poor mental health, including, in extreme cases, the presence of psychosomatic symptoms such as ulcers, nail biting, and insomnia. In addition to being more expressive and less anxious, high self-esteem children tend to communicate a pleasant set of emotions and are less likely to be despondent or unhappy.

Finally, we can conclude that high self-esteem children tend to be dramatically less violent and destructive than low self-esteem children. Children who have poor self-concepts are likely to vent personal hostility against others or against inanimate objects, leading to fighting and the destruction of property.

From this review we can easily conclude that there are important reasons for attending to self-concept enhancement in the middle school. A self-concept improvement program may not raise academic achievement, but it does promise to have other, tangible benefits that are as important to the middle school program as the "basics." In fact, good mental health and a rich emotional life may be the most basic basics of all.

REFERENCES

Bledsoe, J. Self concept of children and their intelligence, achievement, interests, and anxiety, *Childhood Education,* 1964 36-38.

Brookover, W.B.; Thomas, S.; and Patterson, A. Self-concept of ability and school achievement. *Sociology of Education,* 1964 (37), 271-278.

Cappadona, D.L.; Kerzner-Lipsky, D. Prediction of school-mathematical achievement from motivation, self-concept, teachers' ratings and ability measures. *School Science and Mathematics,* 1979, 79(2), 140-144.

Coopersmith, J. *The Antecedents of Self-Esteem,* San Francisco: W.H. Freeman and Company, 1967.

Curtis, R.C.; Zanna, M.P., and Campbell, W.W. Sex, fear of success, and the preceptions and performance of law school students. *American Education Research Journal,* 1975 (12), 287-297.

Kash, M. and Borich, G. *Teacher Behavior and Pupil Self-Concept,* Reading: Addison-Wesley, 1978.

Liska, A.E., ed. The consistency controversy. *Readings on the Impact of Attitude on Behavior.* New York: Wiley, 1975.

Reckless, W.C. and Dinitz, C. Pioneering with self-concept as a vulnerability factor in deliquency, *Journal of Criminal Law, Criminology and Police Science,* 1967 (58). 515-523.

Rosenberg, B.S. and Gaier, E.L. The Self-concept of the adolescent with learning disabilities, *Adolescence,* 1977 (12), 489-498.

Stanwyck, D.J.and Felker, D.W. Intellectual achievement, responsibility and anxiety as functions of self-concept of third to sixth grade boys and girls, Paper presented at AERA, Feb. 4-7, 1973, New York, Eric Repo Service: ED 080903.

Weinstein, Rhonda S. Reading group membership in first grade: teacher behaviors and pupil experience over time, *Journal of Educational Psychology,* 1976 (68), 103-116.

Zimmerman, I.L. and Allenbrand, G.N. Personality characteristics and attitudes toward achievement of good and poor readers, *Journal of Educational Research,* 1965 (59), September, 20-30.

May, 1981

13. Instructional Questions

Students more effectively learn facts, concepts, and principles when they actively think about related information and apply it in a variety of problem solving situations (2, 9). Asking questions is the technique teachers most frequently employ to encourage active information processing. Bellack reported that approximately 45% of what teachers say to students during classroom interactions could be classified as questioning (5). In addition, teachers frequently use written questions to support reading assignments.

ORAL QUESTIONS

The questions teachers ask in class are the best clues students have to determine what they should be learning. Sanders (23) extended Bloom's (6) work on education objectives to develop a comprehensive taxonomy for classifying classroom questions and, in the minds of students, the kind of learning that the teacher is seeking. Sanders described how questions could be formulated to require recalling specific facts, translating given information into different forms, interpreting relationships, applying information to new problem situations, making generalizations, analyzing data, synthesizing several apparently unrelated events to reveal an underlying pattern, and making judgements according to some set of standards. Blosser proposed a less complicated classificaton scheme with four categories: managerial, rhetorical, closed, and open (7). Managerial questions are used to keep classroom operations moving; rhetorical questions emphasize a point or reinforce an idea; closed questions check retention of previously learned information and focus attention on a particular point; open questions promote discussions, stimulate student thinking and allow freedom to hypothesize, speculate and share ideas. Other classification systems have been developed but they do not appear to differ greatly from the above in terms of usefulness to the classroom teacher (1, 25).

Classroom observations indicate that about 60% of the questions teachers ask require the recall of facts (closed questions), about 20% require students to think (open questions), and about 20% are procedural in nature (managerial questions) (13).

On the surface it appears that teachers ask too many fact recall questions and not enough thought provoking, open questions. This may be a warranted conclusion and teachers might improve the quality of student learning by simply asking a greater number of thought provoking questions (10, 16, 17, 24). However, several studies have reported no significant difference in achievement between groups of students who experienced fact-recall and high-order questions (4, 21, 22). In an extensive review of the research relating higher cognitive questions and student achievement, Winne stated that "there is no sturdy conclusion which can be offered about the relative effectiveness of teachers' use of higher cognitive questions for enhancing student achievement" (29). Failure to establish an empirical link, however, was attributed to poorly designed studies and failure to reliably use higher congitive questions with one group and knowledge-recall questions with the other.

Most studies to determine the effect of thought provoking questions simply compare achievement in classes experiencing more higher level questions to classes experiencing fewer. Taba proposed that the sequence in which questions are asked is a critical factor in determining the quality of student learning which results (24). She recommended a sequence that establishes the facts first, followed by questions that require grouping and classifying, interpreting information, making inferences, and finally applying previous knowledge to new situations. The careful sequencing of information processing from less to more abstract representations is necessary to get students thinking at higher levels. The factual-base must be well established before attempts are made to apply the new information in problem solving situations. The higher percentage of closed questions observed in classrooms may not be a problem if *they serve as a foundation for open questions that foster higher-levels of information processing.*

The researchers' message to middle school teachers seems to be that while higher-level open questions may be useful, they should be the final step in a well planned sequence that leads students from recalling information to applying it in problem solving situations.

Students need time to formulate answers to questions. Unfortunately, teachers frequently do not allow adequate time for students to respond, especially when the response calls for reorganizing facts and ideas and applying them to new situations. Classroom observers report that teachers allow an average of *less than one second* for students to respond. When a response is not immediately forthcoming, teachers rephrase the question or redirect it to another student. Rowe reported that increasing wait-times to approximately three seconds resulted in longer student responses, more unsolicited but appropriate responses, fewer failures to respond, greater student confidence, more speculative thinking, more contributions from "slower students", and fewer discipline problems (20). A second important time to pause is *after a student's response.* Teachers tend to immediately confirm or deny the correctness of student responses; if a pause of approximately three seconds is used after a student response, more student input is encouraged and greater information processing is likely to occur (11,20).

The research message regarding teacher wait-time is that silence may be golden. Students need time to think before responding to teacher initiated questions or to answers given by other students. Waiting approximately three seconds after posing a question and after eliciting a student's response should provide adequate thinking time in most classrooms.

WRITTEN QUESTIONS

Increased efficiency of reading guided by questions has been demonstrated by numerous studies (13, 14, 15, 26, 27). However, practical questions remain as to the best use of questions to support written instructional materials. Where should the questions be placed? Do thought-provoking questions result in more learning than those requiring the recall of facts? Do questions restrict learning to information needed to answer the questions or do they possess a general facilitative effect?

Following a study to compare the effects of questions before reading to questions after reading, Washburn concluded that questions placed before the material are more effective than questions following the material (26). However, when Frase investigated the effect of question position, he concluded that questions are more effective if placed after a prose passage (12). Results similar to Frase's have been reported by Bruning (8), Rothkopf (18), and Rothkopf and Bisbicos

(19). Subjects in the studies supporting Frase were not permitted to review the material or questions and all the questions were of the fact-recall type.

No clear cut answer to the problem of the best time to give questions relative to reading assignments emerged from the review of the literature. It is clear, though, that students who answer questions learn more from reading materials than those who do not.

Andre reviewed numerous studies to determine if higher-level questions facilitate productive learning while reading. He concluded that one effect of higher-level questions is to improve student recall of information directly related to the information needed to answer the question (3). Watts and Anderson examined the effect of application-level questions with reading materials and concluded that use resulted in better transfer of the concepts and principles to new examples than the use of knowledge recall questions (28).

These results support the use of higher level questions — particularly questions that require the learner to apply to new information to solve problems.

One effect of written questions which appeared in several studies was to direct attention to specific information, perhaps at the expense of other ideas. When questions are used with a reading assignment, students are likely to learn the information needed to answer the question, but not attent to other parts of the assignment. Teachers need to support reading assignments with questions that address the main ideas to be learned. Otherwise, they may mislead students by focusing attention on unimportant facts not related to the real purpose of the assignment.

In summary, reading assignments are more effective when supported by questions. Questions requiring application of the new information appear to be better than those requiring the recall of facts but it probably does not matter if students are given the questions before or after reading. Questions do direct attention to the information needed to answer them, perhaps at the expense of learning other material in the assigned reading.

REFERENCES

1. Anderson, R.C. How to construct achievement tests to assess comprehension, *Review of Educational Research*, 1972, 42, 145-170.
2. Anderson, R.C. Control of student mediating processes during verbal learning and instruction, *Review of Educational Research*, 1972, 42, 145-170.
3. Andre, T. Does answering higher level questions while reading facilitate productive learning? *Review of Educational Research*, 1979, 49, 280-318.
4. Bedwell, L.E., *The Effects of Training Teachers In Question Asking Skills on the Achievement and Attitudes of Elementary Pupils*, Doctoral Dissertation, Indiana University, 1974.
5. Bellack, A., et al., *The Language of the Classroom*, New York, Teachers College Press 1966, edited by D.G. Hennings, *Mastering Classroom Communication*, Pacific Palisades, California, Goodyear Publishing Company, 1975.
6. Bloom, B.S., M.D. Engelhart E.J. Furst, W.H. Hill, and D.R. Krathwohl (Eds.). *Taxonomy of Educational Objectives: Cognitive Domain*, New York: David McKay, 1956.
7. Blosser, P.E. *How to Ask the Right Question*. Washington, National Science Teachers Association, 1975.
8. Bruning, R.H. Effects of review and test-like events within the learning of prose materials, *Journal of Educational Psychology*, 1968, 59, 16-19.
9. Craik, F.M. and R.S. Lockhart. Levels of processing: a framework for memory research, *Journal of Verbal Learning and Verbal Behavior*, 1972 II, 671-684.
10. Cunningham, R.T., Developing question-asking skills, In J.E. Weigand (Ed.), *Developing Teacher Competencies*, Englewood Cliffs, N.J.: Prentice Hall, 1971.
11. Deture, L.R. Relative effects of modeling on the acquisition of wait-time by preservice elementary teachers and concomitant changes in dialogue patterns. *Journal for Research In Science Teaching*, 1979, 16, 553-562.
12. Frase, L.T. Learning from prose material: length of passage, knowledge of results and position of question, *Journal of Educational Psychology*, 1967, 58, 266-272.

13. Frase, L.T. Some unpredicted effects of different questions upon learning from connected discourse, *Journal of Educational Psychology,* 1968, 59, 197-200.
14. Gall, M.D. The use of questions in teaching, *Review of Educational Research,* 1970, 40, 707-721.
15. Holmes, E. Reading guided by questions versus careful reading and re-reading without questions, *School Review,* 1931, 39, 361-371.
16. Hoover, K.H. *The Professional Teachers Handbook,* Boston: Allyn and Bacon, 1976.
17. Hankins, F.P. *Questioning Strategies and Techniques,* Boston: Allyn and Bacon, 1972.
18. Rothkopf, E.F. and Learning from written materials: an exploration of the control of inspection behaviors by test like events., *American Educational Research Journal,* 1966, 3, 241-249.
19. Rothkopf, E.F. and E. Bisibicos, Selective facilitative effects of interspersed questions on learning from written material, *Journal of Educational Psychology,* 1967, 56-51.
20. Rowe, M.B. Wait, wait, wait, *School Science and Mathematics,* 1978, 78, 3, 207-216.
21. Ryan, F.L. Differential effects of levels of questioning on student achievement. *Journal of Experimental Education,* 1973, 41, 63-67.
22. Ryan, F.L. The effects on social studies achievement of multiple student responding to different levels of questioning, *Journal of Experimental Education,* 1974, 42, 71-75.
23. Sanders, N.M. *Classroom Questions: What Kinds?,* New York, Harper and Row, 1966.
24. Shipley, C.M., M.M. Conn, J.F. Hildebrand, and G.T. Mitchell. *A Synthesis of Teaching Methods.* Toronto: McGraw-Hill-Ryerson, 1972.
25. Taba, H. *Thinking in Elementary School Children,* San Francisco; San Francisco State College, 1964.
26. Washbourne, J.H. The use of questions in social science material, *Journal of Educational Psychology,* 1929, 20, 321-354.
27. Watts, G.H. Effects of prequestions on control of attention in written instruction, *The Australian Journal of Education,* 1973, 18, No. 1.
28. Watts, G.H. and R.C. Anderson, Effects of three types of inserted questions on learning from prose. *Journal of Educational Psychology,* 1971, 62, 387-394.
29. Winne, P.H. Experiments relating teachers' use of higher cognitive questions to student achievement, *Review of Educational Research,* 1979, 49, 13-49.

November, 1980

14. Computer-Assisted Instruction*

Computers. Their use in schools has grown in staggering leaps. The predictions for future access and use are almost beyond comprehension, with some manufacturers anticipating that by the end of this decade there will be as many computers in homes as there are television sets. Computer hardware prices have dropped so dramatically in the past few years, and the software has become so abundant, it is not difficult to understand the manufacturers' optimism.

Educators have not been isolated from all of this activity. The computer, in its many forms, is firmly established in the schools, although definitive answers about the best ways to use it and how effective it is as an instructional tool are elusive. In fact, the research on computer use is scarce; most articles on the subject are devoted to suggestions for use and new technologies. There is also no shortage of commentary on the ways computers can/must/should/will shape the future of education in America. As Jamison (1974) points out, this lack of research is due in part to the enormous technical problems that always accompany the development of new technology; most of the available professional attention has focused on the resolution of these problems, not on scientific study of computer use as a learning tool for young adolescents. In addition, we have discovered that many educators still view computers, even microcomputers, as **research tools,** not as instructional devices about which research needs to be conducted.

Seltzer (1970) reports that computers are used in three principal ways in schools: to conduct drill and practice, to provide tutorial instruction, and to "dialogue" with the student in an interactive way. Drill and practice is activity that is designed to assist the student in **maintaining and enhancing** a skill he has already acquired; tutorials, on the other hand, are programs designed to help a student **acquire** a skill (Vinsonhaler and Bass, 1972). Dialogue is the least common option. It allows a student to enter free-form input to which the computer responds appropriately. It is, quite literally, a conversation (Seltzer, 1970). Zinn (1967) lists other uses as follows: simulation and gaming, retrieval and reorganization of information, problem solving with computation and display tools, and artistic design and composition.

The most important question that educators must ask of computer assisted instruction is "do computers help students learn?"' The answer is generally "yes," but the greatest benefits appear to be in specific types of learning as assessed by specific types of criterion measures.

Computer assisted instruction (CAI) provides the "most individualized interaction between student and the curriculum of any of the methods of instruction yet developed." (Jamison, et al., 1974). But what is the effect of this ultimate form of individualization? Is it what we want for young adolescents?

Computer assisted instruction seems to be especially useful in the skill learning sought via drill exercises. Vinsonhaler and Bass (1972) found that when computer assisted instruction was used to augment teacher instruction they were able to conclude, "...there appears to be strong evidence for the effectiveness of CAI over traditional instructional where effectiveness is measured on standardized achievement tests." There are, however, a number of conditions which must be

Larry C. Holt assisted in the preparation of this report.

considered in modifying this general conclusion. A 1969 study (Suppes and Morningstar) revealed some improvement in scores for third graders in California, but no differences between the CAI augmented experimental group and the non-CAI control group at the sixth grade. However, at the fourth and fifth grade level, traditional methods, those without CAI, produced higher post-test results. It was discovered later that the 4th and 5th grade teachers had, during the study, added 25 minutes a day to the classroom instruction in arithmetic for the fourth and fifth grades. A replication of this study in Mississippi produced much more impressive results. All experimental groups, grades 1-6, scored higher on the post test after receiving CAI drill and practice than did the non-CAI control groups. Two findings are significant here. First, it appears that CAI drill and practice is most effective with students who start out below grade level, as the students in the Mississippi study did. Second, the California study shows that ample and intense effort at classroom drill on the part of the teachers can produce effects as positive as those of the computer.

A 1970 study by Beech (et al.) indicated that there are minimum time expenditures that must be made in order for CAI to be effective, even as a drill procedure. In evaluating the Dial-a-Drill program in New York, Beech and his colleagues found that there was little difference between students in the experimental and control groups because student participation in the voluntary CAI drill and practice program was uneven. Among students who participated in at least 32 sessions (one per week), it was found that those who participated for 15 minutes a week or less (five minute drill sessions three days a week), scored no better than control group students. In other words, 15 minutes of drill a week is not enough; even if it is done on the computer.

After reviewing ten experimental studies of the effects of CAI drill and practice on measures of student achievement, Vinsonhaler and Bass (1972) concluded "most comparisons show an advantage in CAI plus traditional instruction. In a majority of cases, the differences are statistically significant." In fact, the differences between CAI experimental groups and non-CAI controls favored the CAI groups by .10 to .40 of a school year on standardized test scores in Language Arts and by .10 to .88 of a school year in Mathematics. Only one exception to this trend is noted, but it is an important one. In one study, the CAI group scored **lower** on the post-test than did the non-CAI group. This occurred when the outcome measure was The Iowa Test of Basic Skills, rather than The Stanford Achievement Test or The Metropolitan Achievement Test. The investigators explained this phenomenon by pointing out that The Iowa Test measures **concepts** rather than the math **skills** the CAI programs were designed to develop. This suggests that the oldest of curriculum adages is still true: **teach what you test and test what you teach.**

Smith and Hess (1972) studied the effects of CAI on non-cognitive objectives. Students in grades 7, 8, and 9, half of whom were assigned to CAI augmented programs and half of whom received only traditional instruction, were assessed on the following dimensions: control over environment, responsibility for mathematics failure and success, aptitude in math, and social relations. The results indicated no differences between the groups on any of these measures, and no difference between the pre and post-test means of attitude scales administered to the CAI group. At least two studies have noted, though, that students taught through CAI, and who have limited contact with classmates, show lack of growth in social behavior indices and become somewhat estranged from the group (Suppes, 1968; Sears and Feldman, 1968).

Evidently, student attitudes are controlled to some degree by the program of instruction they are given by the computer. While computer assisted instruction has been shown to help with motivating students to learn, particularly in mathematics (Critchfield and Dwyer, 1974; Dwyer 1974, 1977), students quickly lose interest if the computer is not responsive to their control — as is the case in most traditional computer-generated drill lessons. When students use programs over which they have some measure of control, they tend to enjoy mathematics more and improve in their work (Bell, 1978).

To what extent does the novelty effect of working with a computer affect learning outcomes? Vinsonhaler and Bass (1972) suggest that the depressed achievement they noted in the second year of one study of CAI in mathematics "could be due to the loss of a novelty effect of CAI that was present in the first year of the study." A different conclusion is suggested, though, by the work of Atkinson (1968). One hundred students were randomly assigned to experimental and control groups, and the experimental group received CAI tutorial instruction in reading. At the same time, however, the control group received CAI tutorial instruction in math; thus eliminating the possible differential effects of novelty on the two groups. The experimental group outscored the control group by a significant margin on all subtests of both The California Reading Test and The Hartley Reading Test.

One conclusion about which there is little debate, though, is that CAI saves time. Even in cases where there is no difference in the achievement of CAI and non-CAI groups, the CAI group almost always takes **less time** to master a set of material than does a traditionally instructed group. (Axeen, 1967). Bitzer and Boudreaux (1969) found that CAI material from the PLATO system taught complex information in 50 hours, as opposed 84 hours of standard lecture presentations. Homeyer (1970) found that CAI taught students completed course material significantly faster than those in a traditional group, and that there are no differences in the achievement scores of students taught by the two different methods. Further, he discovered that both groups of students make approximately the same number of contacts with the instructor during the course.

As is the case with any complex subject, there are no uniform conclusions that can be drawn with absolute certainty. However, these four generalizations seem to emerge from the research with enough regularity to inspire confidence in their veracity (Gleason, 1981):

1) CAI is most successful in helping learners attain clearly specified objectives, especially in the skill domain.
2) CAI saves significant amounts of time over "conventional" instruction, as much as 20 to 40 percent.
3) Retention rates following CAI are at least as good and often better than retention following conventional instruction.
4) Students have positive attitudes toward good CAI programs and they dislike poor programs, especially those over which they have no control.

In almost all of the studies reported here, the investigation has focused on teacher instruction **augmented** by computer assisted instruction. It is clear that technology can be used to make teachers more effective, but that it cannot replace them. In fact, technology may permit teachers to return to more **traditional** roles; roles that enhance citizenship, encourage critical thinking, pique creativity, and facilitate the exploration of value and moral issues — the things that teachers used to do which seem to have been pushed aside in the back-to-the-basics movement. Technology can help transmit information, teach certain skills, and help students solve problems. Perhaps most important, in doing these things it will free the teacher from being a dispenser of information and permit her to be, once again, an intellectual mentor and personal advisor to our middle grade students.

REFERENCES

Atkinson, R.C. Computerized instruction and the learning process, *American Psychologist,* 23:225-239, 1968.

Axeen, M.E. Teaching the use of the library... Report Number R-361, Urbana: University of Illinois Coordinated Science Laboratory, 1967.

Beech, R.P., S.D. McClelland, G.R. Horowitz and G. Forlano, Final report: an evaluation of the dial-a-drill program, New York: State Department of Education, 1970.

Bell, F.H. Can computers really improve school mathematics? *Mathematics Teacher,* 71:428-433, 1978.

Blitzer, M. and M. Boudreaux, Using a computer to teach nursing *Nursing Forum,* 8, 1969.

Critchfield, M. and T. Dwyer, Computers and the romantic view of education, *Technical Horizons Education,* 1:4-9, September, 1974.

Dwyer, T. Heuristic strategies for using computers to enrich education, *International Journal of Man-Machine Studies,* 6:137-154, 1974.

Dwyer, T. Personal computers in education, Proceedings of the First Far West Computer Fair, San Francisco: Computer Fair, 1977.

Gleason, G.T. Microcomputers in education: the state of the art, *Educational Technology,* 21:3:7-18, March, 1981.

Homeyer, F.C. Development and evaluation of an automated assembly language teacher, Technical Report Number 3, Austin: The University of Texas Computer Assisted Instruction Lab.

Jamison, D., Patrick Suppes and Stuart Wells, The effectiveness of alternative instructional media: a survey, *Review of Educational Research,* 44: 1, 1974.

Sears, P. and D.H. Feldman, Changes in young children's classroom behavior after a year of computer assisted instruction, *Research Memorandum Number 31,* Stanford: Center for Research and Development in Teaching, 1968.

Seltzer, R.A. Computer assisted instruction — what it can and cannot do, *American Psychologist,* 26:373-377, April, 1971.

Smith, I.D. and R.D. Hess, The effects of computer assisted instruction on student self-concept, locus of control, and level of aspiration, Research and Development Memo Number 89, Stanford: Center for Research and Development in Teaching.

Suppes, P. Computer-assisted instruction: an overview of operations and problems, *Proceedings of the IFIP Congress,* 2:1103-1113, 1968.

Suppes, P. and M. Morningstar, Computer assisted instruction, *Science,* 165:343-350, 1969.

Vinsonhaler, J. and R. Bass, A summary of ten major studies of CAI drill and practice, *Educational Technology* 12:29-32, 1972.

Zinn, K. Computer technology for teaching and research on instruction, *Review of Educational Research,* 37:618-634, 1967.

May, 1983

III
Needed Research

1. Priorities for Research in Middle School Education*

Organization and instructional practices employed in middle schools are frequently based upon recommendations of experts in the field, preferences of local administrators, or the political give and take among teachers, administrators, boards of education, and community special interest groups. Implementation of these practices has generated questions which can best be answered through empirical research and/or systematic evaluation of existing programs.

Unfortunately, the present "state of the art" in middle school research is not well developed. There has not been enough research to discern clear-cut trends, although a growing number of individual studies suggest that research based recommendations in the areas of teaching styles and school organization may be possible in the near future. Also, topics for research have been selected on the basis of idiosyncratic interests of individual researchers. Although such a basis is not necessarily bad, it is often difficult to determine where a given research study fits within the scheme of middle school education. A consensus framework identifying broad areas of needed research and specific researchable topics within these areas would facilitate the recognition of patterns of research results and identify gaps in our existing knowledge of middle school practices. Furthermore, practitioners will be more apt to apply research findings when they know where they fit and researchers will be more aware of the productive areas for inquiry if such a "framework of consensus" can be constructed.

The purpose of the present study was to construct a consensus framework of needed research to guide researchers and assist practitioners within the middle school movement.

PROCEDURES

The Delphi technique was employed on a random sample of National Middle School Association members to identify topics of needed research in middle school education and to seek consensus on the usefulness of each research topic. The first step consisted of asking 400 randomly selected NMSA members to identify questions they would like to see answered by middle school research. The responses to this questionnaire were reworded to be grammatically compatible. Research problems mentioned by more than one individual were placed on a new questionnaire along with the number of people naming each item.

For the second round, respondents to the first mailing (n=148) were asked

Jeffry Gordon and David Strahan were co-authors of this article.

to rate the usefulness of each topic on a scale from 1 to 7 (7=very useful and 1=not useful). Mean scores for each of the thirty-six items were computed.

For the third round, respondents to the second questionnaire (n=94) were sent a new questionnaire containing the same thirty-six items, the mean score for the group on each item, and the individual respondent's rating of each item. They were told to reconsider their own rating in light of the group mean, and change their responses if they so desired. Seventy-seven participants responded to this third and final questionnaire.

Means and standard deviations were computed for each item from the final questionnaire. These are reported on Table I. The items were grouped into five broad research areas by three of the four authors.

RESULTS

The seventy-seven returns of the third mailing were examined to determine the extent to which they constituted a reasonable representation of the association's membership. Representing 39 states, the responses came from administrators at the building and central office levels (67%), teachers (22%), and "others," primarily university faculty (11%). Based on available demographics, the sample appears to be reasonable reflection of the association's membership with perhaps a slightly disproportional response from administrators.

Research problems were classified into five broad areas:
1. Organization of the middle school (plans, programs, and staff)
2. Characterizing the middle school student
3. Teaching middle school students
4. Training middle school teachers
5. Obtaining public support for the middle school concept.

Respondents believed that research in the area of middle school organization is needed, particularly with respect to staffing, appropriate curriculum selection, and scheduling. It should not be surprising in the present climate that investigations into curriculum to develop basic skills were rated quite useful (m=5.72) with substantial agreement (s=0.98) among respondents. However, respondents also identified a need for researching exploratory offerings to enrich the core curriculum (m=5.68).

Identifying distinguishing characteristics of middle school versus junior high schools and determining the "best" grade arrangement for a middle school were regarded as less important. Respondents seemed more concerned about what works with students of the middle years than creating a definition per se of the middle school. Perhaps respondents believed that the question of a "definition" has already been adequately explored.

There appears to be a strong need to identify the physiological and psychological development characteristics affecting school performance which are unique to students at this level. The very high usefulness score (m=6.18) and relatively low standard deviation (s=1.08) indicates substantial agreement among respondents on the positive value of research addressing this problem.

High priority should be given to research determining successful teaching techniques for middle grade students. Of particular interest are investigations into successful classroom management procedures (m=6.01). The low standard deviation (s=0.88) indicates substantial agreement by respondents that research in this area would provide worthwide information. Respondents also expressed interest in research to identify and develop successful techniques for motivating students and providing for individual differences.

Research to determine effective preservice and inservice education for middle school personnel received high usefulness ratings by respondents. The high value for research into preservice teacher training in particular (m=5.92) indicates that respondents perceive a need for specialized training at the undergraduate level yet are likely uncertain as to the appropriate nature of such training.

TABLE I
USEFULNESS RATINGS OF 36 IDENTIFIED RESEARCH PROBLEMS IN MIDDLE GRADE EDUCATION

AREA	PROBLEM	MEAN (m)*	S.D.(s)
Organization of the Middle School (Middle school plans)	Evaluating the interdisciplinary approaches currently used in the middle school.	5.18	1.07
	Analyzing the strengths and weaknesses of various middle school daily schedules.	5.06	1.39
	Constructing and evaluating criteria and models for evaluating middle schools.	4.99	1.34
	Comparing existing middle school practices with ideal middle school practices.	4.35	1.25
	Determining the best proportion of the school day to be devoted to exploratory courses as compared to basic courses.	4.32	1.58
	Identifying and validating the attributes which best distinguish middle schools from other school plans.	4.19	1.28
	Determining the most effective size (enrollment) for a middle school and for middle school classes.	3.86	1.34
	Determining the most effective grade organization for middle schools.	3.68	1.42
	Evaluating various middle school building designs and facilities.	3.22	1.26
(Middle school programs)	Developing and evaluating a middle school curriculum that develops basic skills.	5.72	0.98
	Developing and evaluating exploratory offerings that should be included in the middle school curriculum.	5.68	0.85
	Identifying types of activity programs that are most beneficial for middle school students.	5.27	1.30
	Designing and validating a middle school reading program.	5.19	1.31
	Comparing the learning outcomes (cognitive, social affective, psychomotor, etc.) of middle school programs with those of junior high school programs.	5.04	1.44

*Maximum possible rating: 7
Minimum possible rating: 1

	Determining which components of the middle school program prepare students for successful high school performance.	4.92	1.54
	Assessing the effectiveness of various types of athletic programs for middle school students.	4.64	1.46
	Identifying and validating effective strategies for implementing career education in the middle school.	3.88	1.50
(Middle school staff)	Identifying characteristics of successful middle school teachers.	6.18	1.08
	Identifying the characteristics of successful middle school administration.	5.58	1.18
	Identifying and validating a criteria for selecting a middle school staff.	5.09	1.29
Characterizing the Middle School Student	Identifying the unique developmental characteristics which impact on middle school student's learning.	6.19	1.08
Teaching Middle School Students	Analyzing the effects of various management, organizational and disciplinary procedures on student behavior.	6.01	0.88
	Identifying and validating techniques for motivating middle school students.	5.66	1.25
	Analyzing instructional procedures designed to deal with individual differences.	5.56	0.90
	Analyzing and evaluating instructional strategies used in the middle school.	5.41	1.02
	Evaluating the effectiveness of different team-teaching procedures in the middle school.	5.39	1.16
	Analyzing the effects of grouping procedures on academic and social emotional growth.	5.38	1.12
	Identifying and validating systems for assessing and reporting pupil progress.	5.09	1.21
	Evaluating various counseling methods (individual, group, teacher led)	4.97	1.12
	Identifying and validating instruments for evaluating students' cognitive, affective, social and psychomotor development.	4.75	1.26
	Identifying and validating techniques for implementing computer assisted instruction in the middle school.	2.47	1.24
Training Middle School Teachers	Identifying and validating the components of an effective preservice training program for middle school teachers and administrators.	5.92	1.17
	Evaluating procedures for retraining inservice teachers for middle school teaching.	5.69	1.16
	Identifying and validating the components of an effective in-service program for middle school professionals.	5.65	1.21
	Comparing the effectiveness of elementary, secondary, and middle school trained teachers and administrators.	4.34	1.41

| Obtaining public support for the Middle School Concept | Developing procedures to elicit public support for the middle school philosophy. | 4.66 | 1.39 |

Finally, there seemed to be mild interest in how to elicit public support for middle school philosophies. However, the relatively low average (m=4.66), as well as the somewhat high standard deviation (s=1.39 indicating lack of agreement among respondents as to the profitability of this research), should make investigations into this area a lower priority item.

CONCLUSIONS AND RECOMMENDATIONS

Applied research related to practices and procedures that result in more effectively educating middle school students should be emphasized. National Middle School Association members are interested in what "works with students" and "how to do it." There is less concern about comparisons of junior high schools and middle schools. Apparently Wiles and Thomason's (1975) suggestion to study the qualities or practices of middle schooling in an attempt to determine those which have a beneficial impact on students is supported by practitioners in the field. Theoretical research, especially in the area of psychological and physchological development and its impact upon learning, may be useful. The middle school movement, however, has apparently reached the point where empirical investigations of its practices are needed. Curriculum development and evaluation, instructional techniques, staffing procedures and teacher training are areas of potentially useful middle school research.

Where do we go from here...

We believe fundamental questions have been raised which cover the range of researchable areas within the middle school movement. There is, of course, much work to be done. Thorough literature reviews on each of the topics is a beginning step. These reviews might extend into studies done at the elementary and high school levels. Some research, in curriculum for example, may have already been partially completed and reported in subject matter specific journals designed for teachers at all levels. Once the literature has been explored on a particular topic, empirical research, fitting into the consensus framework of what we need to know about middle school education can be carried out.

BIBLIOGRAPHY

Cyphert, F. and Grant, W. The delphi technique: a case study. *Phi Delta Kappan,* 1971, 52:5, pp. 272-273.

Gatewood, Thomas E. What reseach says about the middle school, *Educational Leadership,* 31:221-224, December, 1973.

Gatewood, Thomas E. What research says about the junior high versus the middle school. Paper presented at annual meeting of the North Central Association, Chicago, March 29, 1971.

George, Paul S. Unresolved issues in education for the middle years, *The Clearing House,* 47:417-419, March 1973.

Ruebel, Marion A. Comments on research, *N.A.S.S.P. Bulletin,* 56:86-88, October, 1972.

Skutch, M. and Hall, D. Delphi: potential use in educational planning. Project SIMU-School: Illinois, Chicago component. Chicago Board of Education, July 1973.

Sweigert, R. and Schabacker, W. The delphi technique: how well does it work in setting educational goals. Atlanta, Georgia State Board of Education, April 1974.

Wiles, John H. and Julia Thomason, Middle school research 1968-1974: a review of substantial studies, *Educational Leadership,* 32:421-423, March, 1975.

May, 1980

PUBLICATIONS
NATIONAL MIDDLE SCHOOL ASSOCIATION

The New American Family and the Schools
J. Howard Johnston (48 pages) ISBN 1-56090-047-4 ....$6.00

Who They Are, How We Teach: Early Adolescents and Their Teachers
C. Kenneth McEwin and Julia Thomason (26 pages) $4.00
ISBN 1-56090-046-6

The Japanese Junior High School: A View From the Inside
Paul George with Evan George and Tadahiko Abiko (56 pages) $5.00
ISBN 1-56090-044-X

Schools in the Middle: Status and Progress
Wiliiam M. Alexander and C. Kenneth McEwin (101 pages) $10.00
ISBN 1-56090-043-1

A Journey Through Time: A Chronology of Middle Level Resources
Edward J. Lawton (26 pages) ISBN 1-56090-042-3 ....$5.00

Dynamite in the Classroom: A How-To Handbook for Teachers
Sandra L. Schurr (272 pages) ISBN 1-56090-041-5 ....$15.00

**Developing Effective Middle Schools Through Faculty Participation.
Second and Enlarged Edition**
Elliot Y. Merenbloom (108 pages) ISBN 1-56090-040-7 ....$8.50

Preparing to Teach in Middle Level Schools
William M. Alexander and *C. Kenneth McEwin* (76 pages) $7.00
ISBN 1-56090-039-3

Guidance in the Middle Level Schools: Everyone's Responsibility
Claire Cole (34 pages) ISBN 1-56090-038-5 ....$5.00

Young Adolescent Development and School Practices: Promoting Harmony
John VanHoose and *David Strahan* (68 pages) $7.00
ISBN 1-56090-037-7

When the Kids Come First: Enhancing Self-Esteem
James A. Beane and *Richard P. Lipka* (96 pages) $8.00
ISBN 1-56090-036-9

Interdisciplinary Teaching: Why and How
Gordon F. Vars (56 pages) ISBN 1-56090-035-0 ....$6.00

Cognitive Matched Instruction In Action
Esther Fusco and *Associates* (36 pages) ISBN 1-56090-034-2 ....$5.00

The Middle School
Donald H. Eichhorn (128 pages) ISBN 1-56090-033-4 ....$6.00

Long-Term Teacher-Student Relationships: A Middle School Case Study
Paul George with Melody Spreul and *Jane Moorefield* (30 pages) $4.00
ISBN 1-56090-032-6

Positive Discipline: A Pocketful of Ideas
William Purkey and *David Strahan* (56 pages) $6.00
ISBN 1-56090-031-8

Teachers as Inquirers: Strategies For Learning With and About Early Adolescents
Chris Stevenson (52 pages)   ISBN 1-56090-030-X $6.00

Adviser-Advisee Programs: Why, What, and How
Michael James (75 pages)   ISBN 1-56090-029-6 ....$7.00

What Research Says to the Middle Level Practitioner
J. Howard Johnston and *Glenn C. Markle* (112 pages) $8.00
ISBN 1-56090-028-8

Evidence For the Middle School
Paul George and *Lynn Oldaker* (52 pages) $6.00
ISBN 1-56090-026-1

Involving Parents in Middle Level Education
John W. Myers (52 pages)   ISBN 1-56090-025-3 ....$6.00

Enhancing Learning Through Written and Oral Expression: Strategies for Subject Area Teachers
Ronnie L. Sheppard (112 pages)   ISBN 1-56090-024-5 ....$6.50

Perspectives: Middle School Education, 1964-1984
John H. Lounsbury, editor (190 pages)   ISBN 1-56090-023-7 ....$10.00

Middle School Education: As I See It
John H. Lounsbury (64 pages)   ISBN 1-56090-022-9 ....$5.50

The Theory Z School: Beyond Effectiveness
Paul S. George (106 pages)   ISBN 1-56090-021-0 ....$6.00

The Team Process in the Middle School: A Handbook for Teachers, Second and Enlarged Edition
Elliot Y. Merenbloom (120 pages)   ISBN 1-56090-020-2 ....$8.00

This We Believe
NMSA Committee (24 pages)   ISBN 1-56090-019-9 ....$3.50

Teacher to Teacher
Nancy Doda (64 pages)   ISBN 1-56090-018-0 ....$6.00

The Middle School in Profile: A Day in the Seventh Grade
John H. Lounsbury, Jean Marani, and *Mary Compton* (88 pages) $7.00
ISBN 1-56090-017-2

Early Adolescence: A Time of Change-Implications for Parents
videocassette (37 minutes)   ISBN 1-56090-015-6 ....$75.00

Early Adolescence: A Time of Change-Implications for Schools
videocassette and Utilization Guide (50 minutes) $80.00
ISBN 1-56090-016-4

NMSA, 4807 Evanswood Drive, Columbus, Ohio, 43229-6292
(614) 848-8211   FAX (614) 848-4301